HOME SAUSAGE MAKING

by Charles Reavis

GARDEN WAY PUBLISHING

CHARLOTTE, VERMONT 05445

This book is dedicated to my family,
who make it all worthwhile.

Library of Congress Cataloging in Publication Data

Reavis, Charles, 1948-
    Home sausage making.

    Includes index.
    1. Sausages.   2. Cookery (Sausages)   I. Title.
TX749.R4   641.6'6   80-39703
ISBN 0-88266-246-5

Contents

Acknowledgments

Even though this book has only my name on the cover it belongs in part to the many people who have been so generous with their help, understanding, and encouragement.

Although it is impossible to acknowledge everyone who contributed in one way or another, I owe a special debt of gratitude to the following people: to my mother, Georgia Reavis, who suggested the book in the first place; to Vince Luizzi, friend and philosopher who shares freely his recipes as well as his advice; to my late grandfather, George Lunga, who showed me what it takes to turn a hog into sausages and pork chops; to my editor, Roger Griffith, who has not only had to put up with my idiosyncrasies but has taught me much about the making of a good book; to countless friends who have been more than generous with their ideas and encouragement; and last but never least, to my wife, Jana, and son, Chuck, who have put up with me (and without me) while this book was in the making.

Introduction

Sausage making is one of the (almost) lost arts, but one that's gaining in popularity. When you've smelled a batch of homemade, plump, and juicy sausages sizzling on a grill in your own kitchen you will appreciate the thrill and satisfaction that comes with making your own.

Making your own sausage is easy: I'll show you how.

Making your own sausage is economical: you can use cheaper cuts of meat which you might not ordinarily consider buying. Alternatively, if you have the land and the time you can raise your own meat and reduce the cost of your sausage even further. And, of course, there is always the opportunity to hunt for some of your own meat much like your ancestors did. Venison and other wild game meats make fine sausage.

Making your own sausage is fun: you'll relish the satisfaction that comes from turning out plump, juicy sausages with your own hands.

Making your own sausage is, best of all, better for you. You know exactly what goes into it and the conditions under which you make it are as clean and wholesome as you care to make them.

CHAPTER ONE

The Many Sausages

Making your own sausage will put you in a league with some famous people who, even if they didn't actually make their own, contributed to sausage's sometimes inglorious past.

Although Homer didn't mention anything about Helen of Troy sending out for a sausage and pepperoni pizza, he did state in the *Odyssey* that when the Greeks and Trojans weren't fighting they often enjoyed a few plump, well-turned sausages grilled over the campfire.

Constantine, on the other hand, banned sausage shortly after he inherited the Roman Empire. It seems that he was embarrassed by the orgies at which sausage was often consumed. His puritanical sensibilities simply wouldn't stand for it. Of course he also banned skinnydipping in the public baths so you know that he was just no fun at all.

Our own history might have been different if (so the story goes) Captain John Smith hadn't been so adept at roasting his homemade Polish kielbasa over an open fire. It seems that Pocahontas loved that sausage and so she convinced daddy to spare Captain John's life. And they say the way to a *man's* heart . . . ? Anyway, with a name like Smith it was no easy feat for kielbasa to come to the rescue.

Sausage Varieties

To the best of my knowledge no one has ever catalogued all the various kinds of sausage in the world. The attempt would probably be futile since some sausage is made only in a small region and some kinds of sausage don't exist anymore. The American Indians, for instance, made several kinds of dry or cured sausage from meat and berries but they never bothered to write down their recipes. To further complicate matters every sausage maker has his own — very often secret — recipe for a particular kind of sausage. A generic term like "salami" refers to dozens of different sausages, some no more alike than night and day.

It is for these reasons that there really is no such thing as

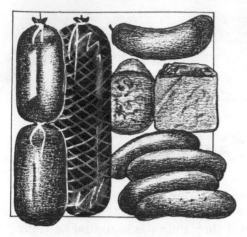

"Italian sausage" or "Polish sausage" or any of the other dozens of ethnic varieties sold in most supermarkets. Certain *kinds* of sausages owe allegiance to various countries or regions but "Italian sausage" may be Italian to one person but pure bologna to another.

By definition (mine), sausage is a mixture of ground meat laced with herbs and spices. That doesn't begin to describe the virtually limitless varieties of sausage.

All sausages fall into one of two groups. Fresh sausages must be cooked before being eaten. They must be treated like other fresh meat — kept cold when stored. Cured sausages are preserved with certain ingredients such as salt and/or they have been dried to prevent spoilage. (See chapter five for a discussion of methods of preservation.) Cured sausages can be eaten as is or with only enough cooking to heat them through.

Fresh Sausages

Let's take a look at the various kinds of sausages we'll be making. First the fresh ones . . . .

Bockwurst is a German-style sausage made from veal or veal and pork. It is usually flavored with onions, parsley, and cloves.

Bratwurst is another German-style sausage made from pork and veal. It looks like a fat hot dog and is delicately flavored with allspice, caraway and marjoram.

Country sausage is one of the most common kinds of sausage found in this country. It can be made into patties or small links and is spiced predominantly with sage.

Frankfurter, or your plain old-fashioned hot dog, is the most widely consumed sausage in the world, thanks primarily to the industriousness of American meat packers. Americans consumed 17 *billion* hot dogs in 1979. Though the commercial variety frank sometimes deserves its lowly reputation, consisting as it does of mostly water and fat, the homemade variety belongs on the same pedestal as all the other homemade sausages because it is just as wholesome and delicious.

Liverwurst is, next to the hot dog, the most famous of the German-style sausages.

Vienna sausage consists primarily of pork and beef, but veal can be added to give it a milder flavor. Onions, mace, and coriander are the predominant flavors.

Cotechino is an Italian-style sausage that is best made from fresh, uncured ham. Nutmeg, cinnamon, and cloves combine with Parmesan cheese to give it its unique flavor.

Luganega is a very mild Italian-style sausage. It is unique in that it is flavored with freshly grated orange and lemon zest.

Northern Italian-style hot or sweet sausage is what you usually see in the meat case labeled simply "Italian sausage." It is traditionally a pure pork sausage in which coriander is the principal herb used as flavoring.

Sicilian-style sausage is basically the same as Northern Italian sausage except that fennel takes the place of coriander.

Chorizo can be either fresh or cured. The fresh variety is similar to Sicilian sausage except that it is much spicier. It is not for people with timid palates.

Garlic sausage can also be fresh or cured. The fresh variety is a pork sausage with lots of garlic and a little white wine for flavor. It is an excellent addition to stews or casseroles that call for some sausage because it is able to stand up to long cooking without losing its flavor.

Polish kielbasa. Like "Italian sausage," kielbasa is more of a generic term than a reference to a specific sausage. The commercial variety is preserved and precooked but the homemade variety is just as often made fresh. I recently had an argument with someone who insisted that the true kielbasa was made solely from pork. In fact, kielbasa can be made from any combination of beef, pork, or veal. Using all three varieties of meat gives the sausage a much more exciting flavor.

Cured Sausages

Cured sausages would take up the most space in any sausage catalogue. The proliferation of this species is due in part to the imaginations of commercial meat-packing plants' promotional departments. Old-time sausage makers were imaginative, to be sure, but the technological *wurstmachers* of today never seem to tire of inventing new varieties — or at least new names for old sausages.

Here are some of the cured sausages we'll be making:

Pepperoni is an Italian-style sausage made from beef and pork. It is quite dry and can be extremely pungent depending upon how much red pepper you dare throw in.

Salami is a generic term that refers to sausages made from beef or pork or both. It comes in many shapes and sizes and can be quite hard and dry.

Garlic sausage, the cured variety, is an extremely complex combination of flavors. It is not meant to be used in recipes calling for garlic sausage (that province rests with the fresh variety) but is intended to be eaten out of hand.

Summer sausage, sometimes called *cervelat*, beefstick, or beer sausage is a beef or pork and beef sausage that resembles some of the drier salamis but has a milder and somewhat sweeter flavor.

Chorizo (dried variety) most closely resembles pepperoni in size and shape but is usually many times more pungent.

Venison sausage is one you'll have to hunt for and your grocer's meat case probably won't have it. It usually includes some pork because, as you know if you've ever tasted venison, it can be very dry if not treated properly.

Thuringer sausage is a German-style, lightly smoked sausage which, though technically cured, is not extremely dry and is more perishable than other cured sausages. Mace, mustard seed, and coriander provide the flavor.

Garlic ring bologna is another "almost cured" sausage that is lightly smoked, precooked, and quite garlicky.

Mettwurst is similar in most respects to garlic ring bologna but is milder in flavor. It contains ginger, celery seed, and allspice.

Braunschweiger is a pure pork German-style sausage. Its flavor is mild and smoky and accented by onions, mustard seed, and marjoram.

Smoked country-style sausage is something you've no doubt encountered in the meat case labeled "little smokies" or something similar. You can easily make your own with pork and beef.

Smoked kielbasa is the sausage you find in the meat case labeled "Polish sausage." It is similar to the fresh variety except that the flavors are more concentrated because it is smoked and precooked.

Bavarian summer sausage is a German-style salami which is indebted to me for its name, because whenever I have some I can't help but think of Bavarian beer fests and rye bread. It is very mildly flavored with mustard seed and sugar.

Yirtrničky is a Czech sausage most easily made if you have access to freshly butchered pork because its ingredients include the meat from a pig's head along with the lungs, heart, and kidneys.

CHAPTER TWO

Equipment and Ingredients

The French have a term for culinary preparedness: *mise en place*. This means that you should have everything gathered together and "in its place" before you start any recipe. Fortunately you probably already have the equipment you'll need, with possibly one or two exceptions, in your kitchen.

Grinders

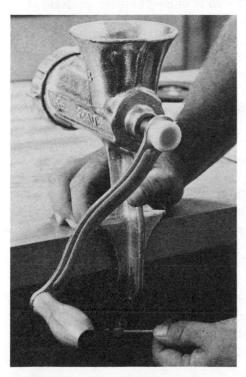

My grinder gets a firm grip on our kitchen counter.

Unless you are a graduate of the Japanese Culinary Institute and are able to wield two razor-sharp knives like a samurai warrior (without losing any fingers in the process), you are going to need something with which to grind the meat. Devices for accomplishing this task range from the simple to the complex and from dirt cheap to outrageously expensive.

An old-fashioned hand grinder, like the one in your grandmother's kitchen, is still a bargain even at today's inflated prices. A good one, with fine and coarse chopping disks, costs less than $20.

The newer plastic model grinders are certainly more attractive than the older metal ones but many of these have suction cup bases for attaching to the kitchen table or counter. Generally these bases are inferior to a heavy-duty clamp-on base, which is standard with most metal grinders. Grinding meat by hand is the most arduous task of the home sausage maker. A suction cup base can lose its suction at very inappropriate times. Don't compound the difficulty of an already laborious task by using a grinder that has to be repositioned every five minutes.

The old metal base grinders are still available in hardware stores and gourmet cooking supply shops and are virtually indestructible. Ours has been in the family for more than four generations. Unless you are going to be making fifty or sixty pounds of sausage at a time, a hand grinder will do the job.

If you don't have access to a family heirloom hand grinder and wish to buy one, there are certain things that you should look for. Make sure that the grinder comes with at least two chopping disks: a fine disk with holes about an eighth of an inch in diameter, and a coarse disk, with holes at least three-eighths of an inch in diameter. Look for a model with a heavy-duty screw clamp for attaching to a table or counter top. It's better to spend a couple of extra dollars in the beginning for a quality appliance than to regret not doing so later when the base collapses while grinding a batch of sausage. One model with which I am familiar (in addition to our family relic) is distributed by Rowoco, Inc. and has five cutting disks and a self-sharpening blade in addition to a heavy-duty base clamp. It is available for less than $30 in many stores where cooking supplies are sold, and should last a lifetime.

Power Grinders

Here are four sizes of disks commonly used in making sausage.

If you don't want to expend the elbow grease needed to grind meat by hand or you plan to make huge batches, an electric food grinder is a good investment. Expect to pay more for the convenience of an electrical appliance: $40 is about rock bottom and professional models cost as much as $400 or $500. Again, choose one that has two or more cutting disks for coarse and fine jobs. All name-brand electric grinders have motors powerful enough to grind meat but some of the more inexpensive models have a tendency to overheat and shut down if more than ten pounds of meat are ground without allowing the unit to cool. Generally speaking the higher the price the more powerful the unit. A moderately priced unit, one in the $60-$80 range, with a motor rated at least one-sixth horsepower, would probably be sufficient for most home sausage makers.

The latest appliance for the cook who has everything, and one that is rapidly gaining a reputation of being indispensable, is the food processor. This machine can serve the home sausage maker admirably. It will chop meat finely, coarsely, or anywhere in between. Its major drawback is that the novice tends to over-process everything. Within a few seconds one-inch cubes of meat can be reduced to something resembling toothpaste. If you already own a food processor by all means use it, but don't feel you must rush out and buy one just to make sausage.

An alternative to grinding your own meat is to have your butcher grind it for you. There are two drawbacks to this, one economic and one practical. After you choose the meat that you want ground, the butcher may charge you extra for boning and grinding it. In the long run a surcharge of ten or twenty cents per pound is going to add up, so putting off buying a grinder will prove a false economy.

Another drawback is that it just will not do to have your beef ground in a machine that the butcher recently used to grind uncertified pork. There's the possibility of trichinosis contamination. (See chapter five for a discussion of ways of avoiding this problem.)

Sausage Funnel

If your grinder doesn't have a sausage stuffing attachment you will have to purchase a sausage funnel. An ordinary kitchen funnel doesn't have an opening large enough to allow the ground meat to pass through easily. Further, the taper is usually such that it doesn't allow you to gather up enough sausage casing at one time to be practical. Sausage funnels come in various sizes and can usually be found in butcher supply stores and restaurant supply shops, or can be ordered through the mail. (See the list of suppliers at the end of the book.) The good thing about these funnels, regardless of where you happen to find them, is that they are relatively cheap.

Old-fashioned but still very practical is this sausage stuffer.

Casings

Casings are packaged this way, and look dry and stringy when first taken from the container.

Sausage has to be stuffed into something, and that something is most often the intestine of a hog, cow, or sheep. Before you gasp, rest assured that these casings are scrupulously cleaned and are packed in salt, which keeps them fresh indefinitely.

These natural casings come in an array of sizes, ranging from under one inch to a little over four inches in diameter. The smallest are usually sheep casings, 1/2 to 1 1/16 inches and the largest are from beef, 2 1/2 to 4 inches. Think of sheep casings as being the size of most hot dogs, and beef casings the size of a large salami. The hog casings are the most common since many fresh sausages are made in the two-inch diameter range. All casings should be kept refrigerated or frozen until ready to use.

You should be familiar with two other types of casing: collagen and muslin. Collagen casings are made of natural, edible pure protein. They generally cost a little more than intestines, are sometimes a little harder to find, but are convenient to use and may be substituted freely for a natural casing in any recipe in this book. Follow the directions that come packed with them.

Muslin casings can be purchased or homemade and are used with summer sausage and salami. One needn't be a Betsy Ross to stitch up a muslin casing. Just follow the instructions in chapter four.

Virtually every meat packing company sells hog, sheep, and beef casings, and if your butcher doesn't stock them he can order them for you. Many grocery stores, especially in ethnic neighborhoods, carry a full line of casings. These too can be ordered by mail if you have difficulty finding them in your area. For most sausage we recommend the natural casings.

Ingredients

In making your own sausages, be they hot dogs or salami, you choose not only the cut of meat but the quality as well.

The pork cuts we'll use are the butt (sometimes called the Boston butt or shoulder roast) and fresh hams. On occasion you might find a rib end loin roast that substitutes admirably for the butt when the price is right or if you are raising your own meat, since these two are adjoining cuts of meat. All three cuts have almost perfect fat-to-lean ratios for making sausage.

In recipes calling for beef and veal the chuck, rump, and shank are the most economical cuts. Since most retailers sell only USDA "choice" beef and veal you can be assured of the quality.

Whether you buy your sausage meat or raise and butcher your own there is one cardinal rule that must be followed faithfully: all meat for sausage must be *very, very* fresh. Grinding creates a proportionately greater surface area in relation to the weight of the meat. The more surface area, the bigger the breeding ground for bacteria. All meat contains bacteria, some good, some bad, some innocuous. Under optimum conditions these bacteria are not allowed to reproduce and taint the sausage.

Extenders

Sausage extenders include soy protein concentrate, soy flour, and powdered skim milk. There is a common misconception that these are added to sausage to "extend" the meat at a lower price. This isn't necessarily the case. Extenders are added by those who believe they make the sausage more moist and juicy. The amount used is very small, about three and one-half pounds per 100 pounds of meat. That's about two tablespoons per pound of meat.

Spices and Herbs

Spices and herbs form a tiny part of the complete mix of a sausage, yet they in large part decide the success of the recipe. For this reason, buy the best, store spices in as dark and as cool a place as possible, date the containers, and throw away all ground spices after a year, since they will have lost much of their strength by that time. Spices stored in shaker-type containers and paper boxes lose their strength far faster than those in closed containers.

Cures

We will save our words on the nitrate question until chapter five, but at this point we wish to point out that among the ingredients used by some in making sausage are concentrated chemicals mixed and sold as cures. They are used to avoid botulism poisoning, to improve the flavor, and to turn the color of the meat to an appealing pink.

Two common cures are Prague Powder #1, a general-purpose sausage and meat cure containing sodium nitrate, and Prague Powder #2, a cure for dry meats, containing sodium nitrate and sodium nitrite. Half a pound of such a powder is used for 200 pounds of meat.

Knives

My preference is a carbon steel knife. I can sharpen it to perfection with my butcher's steel.

The most universal kitchen/cooking utensil is the knife. It is easily the single most important piece of equipment you'll be using because so much of the job involves cutting, boning, and trimming the meat that will be ground into your homemade sausage. The best tool is a knife, or better yet a set of knives, that can be honed to a razor's edge and will stay that way.

There are four kinds of knives on the market: high carbon steel, carbon steel, stainless steel, and those weapons advertised on television that are supposedly equally adept at cutting through tomatoes and tin cans. I wouldn't allow one of those in my kitchen under any circumstances, if for no other reason than I don't want people to think that I have a need for something that cuts through tin cans.

Stainless steel knives are the most popular, easiest to keep clean, and always look shiny. Manufacturers have told the homemaker that stainless steel stays sharper longer. This is probably true, but once it loses its edge a professional knife sharpener must restore it. Next to the implement of destruction mentioned above, stainless should be your last choice in cutlery.

Carbon steel knives can be honed to an extremely keen edge. Because they are not as hard as stainless steel they lose their edge much more rapidly, but it can be restored to perfection with a few swipes over a butcher's steel. They tarnish very easily. When working with meats this doesn't present a major problem. If you should use the knife on any type of acidic food, however, such as onions or garlic, the surface of the knife will blacken and often impart an unpleasant aroma and taste to the food you are cutting.

The most expensive kitchen knives you can buy, and the best, are made of high carbon steel. They marry the best features of carbon and stainless steel knives: they don't tarnish and their edges can be honed and restored in seconds to surgical sharpness. They are made to last a lifetime. The few extra dollars spent on quality will mean dividends in time and energy saved. Using exclusively high carbon steel knives means less time spent keeping the edge sharp, the tarnish and rust off and, when faced with a twenty-pound mound of meat, no sore muscles from trying to hack your way through it with an imperfect knife.

When buying knives, consider what type of knife or knives you'll need. A boning knife aids the meatcutter in getting all the meat possible from a pork butt or beef chuck. It is a good knife to become familiar with, although some people are more comfortable with a smaller paring knife. For slicing, an eight- or ten-inch chef's knife is probably your best bet. Its balance and shape are designed to make the job go quickly with the least amount of effort on your part.

Butcher's Steel

One other tool that should be in every meat cutter's kitchen is a butcher's steel. Nothing more than a steel or ceramic rod with a handle, it is a necessity for sharpening. Manual or electric knife sharpeners grind away the blade. The steel, like a barber's strop, aligns the molecules on the very edge of the blade to create the sharpest possible cutting edge. Expect to pay about $15 for a quality steel.

Remember that a dull knife is a dangerous knife. When you *force* a dull knife to do the job it was intended to do, your hand may slip. Don't compromise on the quality of your knives; keep them honed to precision; take care of them, and they will reward you with easy and safe performance for a lifetime.

CHAPTER THREE

Making Your First Batch

We're ready to make some country-style sausage links. Once you have mastered these techniques you will be able to follow any recipe in this book. But before we begin this three-step procedure — preparing the casing, preparing the meat, and stuffing the sausage — you'll need to assemble the following for three pounds of sausage.

4 feet small hog or sheep casing
2 1/4 pounds lean pork butt, cut into one-inch cubes
3/4 pound pork fat, cut into one-inch cubes
3 teaspoons coarse (kosher) salt
3/4 teaspoon finely ground white or black pepper
1/2 teaspoon dried thyme
1 1/2 teaspoons dried sage
1/4 teaspoon dried summer savory
3/4 teaspoon sugar (optional)
1/2 teaspoon crushed red pepper

It's Next to Godliness

When making sausage, you're taking on the responsibility of providing a food that's both delicious to eat and safe to eat.

Here are some rules to follow:

1. Scrub with hot water all surfaces that will be in contact with the meat. Be particularly careful with your cutting board.

2. Assemble your utensils and equipment: grinder, sausage funnel, knives, mixing spoons, and a large pan for mixing.

3. Sterilize the utensils and the parts of the grinder that will come in contact with the meat by pouring boiling water over them.

4. Remove your rings and wash your hands carefully. Wash them again if you're called away from your work, such as for a phone call.

You're ready to begin.

Preparing the Casing

1 *Snip off about four feet of casing. Better too much than too little because any extra can be repacked in salt and used later. Rinse it under cool running water to remove any salt clinging to it. Place it in a bowl and let it soak for about half an hour . . .*

2 *After soaking, rinse under cool running water . . .*

3 *Slip one end of the casing over the faucet nozzle. Hold it firmly on the nozzle, then turn on the cold water, gently at first, and then more forcefully . . .*

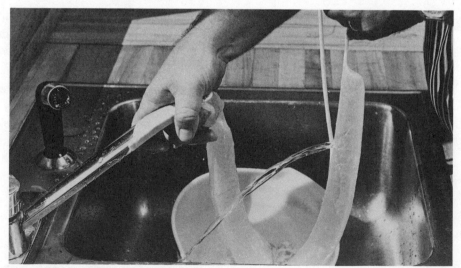

4 *This will flush out any salt in the casing and pinpoint breaks such as this one . . .*

5 *Should you find such a break, cut out that section, and tie off the ends later...*

6 *Place the casing in a bowl of water. Add a tablespoon of vinegar per cup of water to soften the casing a bit more and make it more transparent, which in turn makes the sausage more pleasing to the eye. Leave the casing in the water/vinegar until you use it. Rinse and drain before stuffing.*

Preparing the Meat

7 *Cut the chilled pork butt into one-inch cubes, as I'm doing here. Trim off and save the fat. Refrigerate the cubes and fat for about a half-hour to firm them up before grinding...*

8 *Put the meat through the fine disk (1/4" or smaller), then...*

9 *add the seasonings, . . .*

10 *mix them in with your hands, and grind again through the same disk. If you are using a food processor, process the meat to a very fine dice and mix in the seasonings last. If you are using an electric grinder with a stuffing attachment, sprinkle the seasoning over the meat and mix with your hands before grinding, since the grinding and stuffing will be one operation.*

Stuffing the Sausage

11 *Slide the casing over the sausage funnel or the electric grinder's attachment. Push it along until it is all on the funnel and the end is even with the funnel opening.*

12 *With either an electric grinder or sausage funnel, force the ground meat through until it is flush with the tube opening, then pull off two inches of casing, and tie a simple knot.*

13  *Stuff the casing until all the meat has been used. Feed through small amounts of meat at a time, packing the casing firmly but not to the bursting point. Maintain an even thickness, and avoid trapping air in the casing. When all the meat has been used remove any leftover casing from the funnel.*

14 *Beginning at the tied end of the casing, grasp about three inches of sausage and give it two or three twists in the same direction. This forms a link.*

15 *Continue twisting until all are done. They should look like this.*

16 *With a sharp knife cut the links apart, and cut off the empty casing at the end. The mixture won't squeeze out.*

Cooking

17 *Because it contains raw pork, sausage must be cooked slowly and thoroughly. Patties can be pan fried. With sausages such as we have just made, simmer or steam them for five minutes, then...*

18 *...slowly brown in vegetable oil, broil, or grill.*

Before Eating

Sausage tastes better if it ages so that the herbs and spices can penetrate the meat more completely. Arrange the links in a single layer on a platter and refrigerate them for a couple of hours.

If you are not going to eat them within two days, wrap the links individually in waxed paper and pack them into a plastic bread bag or freezer container and freeze. Frozen sausages will hold their flavor for about eight to twelve weeks. Thaw them completely before cooking. Cook them as thoroughly as you would any fresh pork sausage, and use them in one of your favorite recipes or in one of the recipes in chapter seven.

CHAPTER FOUR

Fresh Sausage Recipes

Now that you have made your first batch of homemade sausage you're ready to try any of the recipes for fresh sausage in this chapter. The techniques for making any kind of fresh sausage are basically the same.

If your family has a favorite sausage try that one next. You'll be able to compare your results with the commercial variety and judge just how superior your own sausage is.

In this chapter one thing is conspicuous by its absence: a preservative. If you look at the label of ingredients on a package of fresh sausage on your grocer's shelf you may find, among other things, potassium sorbate, lactic acid, BHA, BHT, or even one of the nitrate compounds. We'll discuss chemical preservatives in the next chapter, but for now we'll say that under ideal conditions there is no logical reason for adding any kind of chemical preservative to fresh sausage. Commercially prepared fresh sausage products often have preservatives added to them in order to preserve their color and flavor and, by retarding rancidity, give them a longer shelf life.

Homemade sausage is pure sausage. It is made fresh to be cooked and eaten fresh. If it is not to be consumed within a couple of days, it can be frozen. But in no case do preservatives enter the picture.

One more word about the recipes in this chapter — or any recipe in this book for that matter: they are intended to be guides. Every one of them has provided us with much dining pleasure. But don't be afraid to experiment with them. Make them my way the first time. Get a feel for the various combinations of ingredients and how they accent or contrast with one another. The next time you make the same recipe try making small changes in the variety or amounts of the herbs and spices to suit you and your family's tastes. Personalize the recipes and then you can honestly say you've made homemade sausage. Furthermore, if you find yourself with a large amount of meat, the result of butchering a hog, for instance, don't be afraid to double or triple the recipes. In this case you might want to season the meat and cook up a small portion of it to test the seasonings and adjust them if necessary.

German Wursts

Wurst means sausage and is a good place to start because the Germans are probably responsible for more varieties of sausage than any other group of people in the world. Here are some of our favorites.

BOCKWURST

This recipe makes two pounds of this German favorite.

2 feet 1 1/2-inch sausage casings
1 1/2 pounds veal, cubed
1/4 pound pork fat, cubed
1/4 cup very finely minced onion
1 cup milk
1 egg
3/4 teaspoon ground cloves
1/2 teaspoon freshly ground white pepper
1 teaspoon finely chopped Italian (broadleaf) parsley
1 teaspoon salt

1. Prepare the casings. (See chapter three.)
2. Grind the veal and pork fat separately through the fine disk of the grinder. Mix them and grind them again. (If you are using an electric grinder or food processor follow the basic instructions in chapter three for these appliances. All recipes will assume you are using a hand grinder so you should make any changes in procedure yourself.)
3. Add the onion, milk, egg (well beaten), cloves, pepper, parsley, and salt to the meat and mix well.
4. Put mixture through the fine blade of the grinder.
5. Stuff mixture into the casings and twist off into three- or four-inch links. The sausage may be refrigerated for two days or so or may be boiled for thirty minutes and eaten immediately.

BRATWURST

Bratwurst resemble fat hot dogs and at least one company manufactures a preservative-free variety. You can go the commercial version one better by following this recipe for three pounds.

3 feet 1 1/2-inch sausage casings
2 pounds pork butt, cubed (include the marbled fat)
1 pound veal, cubed
1/4 teaspoon ground allspice
1/2 teaspoon caraway seeds
1/2 teaspoon dried marjoram
3/4 teaspoon freshly ground white pepper
1 1/2 teaspoons salt

1. Prepare the casings. (See chapter three.)
2. Grind the veal and pork separately through the fine blade of the grinder.
3. Mix the ground meats and grind again.
4. Add the remaining ingredients to the meat mixture and mix thoroughly.
5. Stuff the mixture into the casings and twist off into four- or five-inch links.
6. Refrigerate for up to two days, if not eating it immediately. The bratwurst can be pan fried or grilled over charcoal. Freeze if not used within two days.

FRANKFURTER

The lowly hot dog is probably the most widely consumed sausage in the world. Its somewhat scurrilous reputation stems from the fact that the commercial product is, to varying degrees, loaded with fat, cereal binders, and chemicals. The commercial hot dog is a nutritional nightmare.

This doesn't have to be the case.

This version of the hot dog doesn't look rosy red like the tube steaks in the grocery store because it doesn't contain any nitrates or coloring agents. (If you would like a little pink in your meat you could add a little vitamin C; see the next chapter for how and why.) Recipe makes two pounds.

3 feet sheep, small hog, or 1-inch collagen casings
1/4 cup very finely minced onion
1 small clove garlic, finely chopped
1 teaspoon finely ground coriander
1/8 teaspoon dried marjoram
1/4 teaspoon ground mace
1/4 teaspoon finely ground mustard seed
1 teaspoon paprika
1 teaspoon freshly fine ground white pepper
1 egg white
1 1/2 teaspoons sugar (optional, but most people are accustomed to having their hot dogs rather sweet)
1 1/2 teaspoons salt
1/4 cup milk
1/2 pound pork fat, cubed
1 pound lean pork, cubed
1/2 pound lean beef, cubed

1. Prepare the casings. (See chapter three.)
2. With a mortar and pestle, or in a blender or food processor, make a puree of the onion, garlic, coriander, marjoram, mace, mustard seed, and paprika.
3. Add the pepper, egg white, sugar, salt, and milk, and mix thoroughly.
4. Spread the pork fat cubes on a cookie sheet and place them in the freezer for half an hour. They grind more easily if well chilled.
5. Grind the pork, beef, and fat through the fine blade separately. Mix and grind them again.
6. This next step is rather sticky so hold your hands under cold running water and leave them wet for mixing. Mix the pureed seasonings and ground meat thoroughly with your hands.
7. Chill the mixture for half an hour, then put the mixture through the fine blade of the grinder once more.
8. Stuff the casings and twist them off into six-inch links.
9. Parboil the links (without separating them) in gently simmering water for twenty minutes.
10. Place the franks in a bowl of ice water. Chill thoroughly.
11. Remove, pat dry, and refrigerate. Because they are precooked they can be refrigerated for up to a week or they can be wrapped and frozen.

LIVERWURST

Liverwurst is one of the most popular of all the German sausages. A thick slice sandwiched between two slices of homemade bread, topped with a slice of Bermuda onion, and lathered with mayonnaise is, if not a feast, at least a wickedly delicious lunch or snack.

This recipe is slightly different from the previous ones in that we don't use animal casings. You will need a piece of unbleached muslin about twelve inches long and eight inches wide. Or you can use wide collagen or fiber casings.

Fold the muslin lengthwise and tightly stitch a seam across one of the short ends and continue down along the open long side. Try to keep the stitching about an eighth of an inch from the edge of the material. The short side seam can be curved in a semicircle and then trimmed to give the finished product a rounded end. Turn the casing inside out so that the stitching is on the inside. Set it aside until you are ready to stuff it.

This recipe makes a two-pound liverwurst.

1 pound fresh pork liver, cubed
3/4 pound lean pork butt, cubed
1/4 pound pork fat, cubed
1 large sweet white onion, finely diced
3 tablespoons powdered dry milk
1 teaspoon freshly fine ground white pepper
2 teaspoons salt
2 teaspoons paprika
1 teaspoon sugar
1/2 teaspoon marjoram
1/2 teaspoon finely ground coriander
1/4 teaspoon mace
1/4 teaspoon allspice
1/4 teaspoon cardamom, ground

1. Put the cubes of liver, pork, and fat through the fine disk of the grinder separately and then mix and grind together.
2. Sprinkle the remaining ingredients over the ground meat and mix thoroughly with your hands.
3. Put the mixture through the fine blade of the grinder twice more, chilling the mixture for a half hour between grindings.
4. Pack the mixture into the muslin casing. It helps to fold the open end back down over itself to get things started. This makes it easier to reach the bottom. Pack the meat as firmly as possible.
5. Stitch the open end closed or firmly secure the end with a wire twist tie.
6. In a large kettle bring to a boil enough water to cover the liverwurst by two or three inches.
7. Put the sausage in and place a weight on it to keep it submerged. Two or three large dinner plates work just fine.
8. When the water returns to a boil reduce the heat so that the water is *barely* simmering.
9. Cook for three hours.
10. Drain out the hot water and replace it with an equal quantity of ice water.
11. When the liverwurst has cooled, refrigerate it overnight and then remove the muslin casing.
12. Store the liverwurst in the refrigerator and eat it within ten days.

VIENNA SAUSAGE

Vienna sausages are traditionally a beef and pork combination. The recipe calls for the addition of some veal to give the sausage a mildly sweet flavor. For three pounds of sausage:

3 feet sheep, small hog, or 1-inch
   collagen casings
1 pound lean pork, cubed
1 pound lean beef, cubed
1/2 pound veal, cubed
1/2 pound pork fat, cubed
2 tablespoons finely minced onion
1 teaspoon sugar
1/2 teaspoon cayenne red pepper
1 teaspoon paprika
1/2 teaspoon finely ground mace
1 1/2 teaspoons finely ground
   coriander
3 teaspoons salt
1/4 cup plus one tablespoon flour
1/2 cup cold milk
1/2 cup cold water

1. Prepare the casings. (See chapter three.)
2. Grind the meats and fat separately through the fine blade of the grinder and mix together.
3. Mix all the remaining ingredients with the meat.
4. Put the mixture through the fine disk.
5. Stuff the casings and twist off into four-inch links. Do not separate the links.
6. Place the links in a kettle and cover with water. Bring to a boil, reduce heat, and barely simmer for forty-five minutes.
7. Remove the links, cool in cold water, pat dry, and refrigerate. They are excellent grilled over an open fire or they can be reheated in boiling water for ten minutes. Use within ten days or freeze.

Italian-Style Sausages

Virtually every grocery store that has a meat case has something in it called Italian sausage. To most Italians many of these so-called Italian sausages are more laughable than edible. To be sure, there are small ethnic neighborhood delicatessens that make the real thing and make it very well indeed. But in many parts of the country these places are hard to find.

The tantalizing aroma of an Italian sausage grilling over an open fire is inspiration enough for a poet. A roasted link, wrapped in a slice of crusty homemade bread and smothered with sautéed onions and sweet peppers, spurting juice on the first bite, is almost sinfully delicious.

Here are four recipes, all family favorites.

COTECHINO

The best cut of meat to use to make cotechini is a fresh ham, because part of the flavor and texture of this sausage depends on pork skin with which this cut of meat is usually marketed. The next time fresh hams are on sale at your local grocery, or you slaughter a pig, try this recipe for six pounds.

4-5 feet 1 1/2-inch hog casings
5 pounds lean fresh ham, cubed
1 pound pork skin with fat, cubed
6 teaspoons salt
4 teaspoons coarse freshly ground
   black pepper
2 teaspoons ground nutmeg
2 teaspoons ground cinnamon
1 teaspoon cayenne red pepper
1 teaspoon finely ground cloves
1/4 cup freshly grated Parmesan
   cheese

1. Prepare the casings. (See chapter three.)
2. Grind the meat and skin coarsely.
3. Mix the remaining ingredients with the meat and grind through the fine disk.
4. Stuff the mixture into casings and twist off into six- or eight-inch links.
5. Separate the links and allow them to dry, uncovered, in the refrigerator for two days. Turn them often so that they dry evenly.
6. You can boil them for forty-five minutes and eat them, or boil, cool, and pack into canning jars. Pour hot melted fat or lard over them to cover, and store them in the refrigerator for up to a month. To use, scoop the sausages out of the jar and reheat them in the lard that clings to the links.

NORTHERN ITALIAN-STYLE
HOT OR SWEET SAUSAGE

This variety is extremely simple to make and is delicious roasted or used to flavor tomato sauce. To make three pounds:

3 feet medium hog casings
2 1/2 pounds lean pork butt, cubed
1/2 pound pork fat, cubed
3 teaspoons coarse salt
2 teaspoons coarsely ground fresh
   black pepper
2 teaspoons finely ground coriander
2 cloves garlic, finely minced
1 teaspoon or more, to taste,
   crushed red pepper for hot sausage

1. Prepare the casings. (See chapter three.)
2. Grind the meat and fat together through the coarse disk.
3. Mix the remaining ingredients with the meat.
4. Stuff into casings and twist off into three-inch links.
5. Refrigerate and use within three days, or wrap links separately and freeze.

LUGANEGA

Luganega is the mildest Italian sausage you will encounter. It is Northern Italian in origin and in this country you would be lucky to find it anywhere except in the kitchen of an Italian home. To make four pounds of luganega:

4 feet medium hog casings
3 pounds lean pork butt, cubed
1 pound pork fat, cubed
1 cup freshly grated Parmesan
   cheese
1/2 teaspoon freshly grated nutmeg
1/2 teaspoon finely ground coriander
1/2 teaspoon grated lemon peel
1/2 teaspoon grated orange peel
1 teaspoon freshly fine-ground
   black pepper
1 small clove garlic, finely chopped
3 teaspoons salt
1/2 cup dry vermouth

1. Prepare the casings. (See chapter three.)
2. Grind the pork and fat together through the fine disk.
3. Sprinkle the remaining ingredients over the meat and mix well.
4. Stuff the mixture into casings and twist off into eight- or ten-inch links.
5. Separate the links and allow them to dry in a cool place for two or three hours.
6. Refrigerate and use within two or three days or wrap separately and freeze. (The flavor of the lemon and orange is intensified by freezing, so the sausage is best when used fresh.)

SICILIAN-STYLE SAUSAGE

This sausage can be made either hot or sweet depending upon whether you add crushed red pepper. If you choose to add the hot pepper let your conscience be your guide.

For five pounds of sausage:

5 feet medium hog casings
4 pounds lean pork butt, cubed
1 pound pork fat, cubed
5 teaspoons coarse salt
3 teaspoons fresh black pepper,
   coarsely ground
2 cloves garlic, finely minced
2 1/2 teaspoons fennel seed
1 teaspoon anise seed
Crushed red pepper to taste

1. Prepare the casings. (See chapter three.)
2. Grind the meat and fat together through the coarse disk.
3. Mix the remaining ingredients with the ground meat and fat.
4. Stuff the mixture into casings and twist off into three- or four-inch links.
5. Refrigerate and use within three days, or wrap sausages individually and freeze.

Other Fresh Sausages

Every nation has its favorite sausage or sausages. Here are recipes for a few of them. Try one or two and you'll understand why they have become so popular.

CHORIZO

In Spain you can find chorizos both fresh and dried. Either way they are hot spicy sausages that sometimes scare away people with timid palates. Try them at least once and you'll be glad you did. To make four pounds of chorizos:

5 feet medium hog casings
3 pounds lean pork butt, cubed
1 pound pork fat, cubed
4 teaspoons coarse salt
2 teaspoons fresh black pepper, coarsely ground
4 teaspoons cayenne pepper, finely ground
1 teaspoon red pepper, coarsely ground
3 large cloves garlic, finely chopped
3 teaspoons red wine vinegar
1/4 cup dry red wine
2 tablespoons brandy
1 teaspoon fennel seed

1. Prepare the casings. (See chapter three.)
2. Grind the meat and fat together through the coarse disk.
3. Mix the remaining ingredients into the ground meat with your hands.
4. Place the mixture in a large covered pan in the refrigerator for three or four hours. This gives the wine and brandy a chance to extract the flavor from the herbs and spices and for the meat to absorb some of the liquid.
5. Stuff the casings and twist off into three- or four-inch links. Refrigerate and use within three or four days, or freeze.

FRESH POLISH KIELBASA

Recipes for this sausage are so varied that what passes for kielbasa in one area might fail the authenticity test in another. The ingredients and pronunciation of kielbasa are as variable from household to household as are the vagaries of the spring weather, the time when kielbasa is traditionally made. This version uses pork, beef, and veal and makes five pounds.

6 feet 2-inch hog casings
3 pounds lean pork butt, cubed
1 1/2 pounds beef chuck, cubed
1/2 pound veal, cubed
6 teaspoons coarse salt
4 teaspoons fresh black pepper, finely ground
1 1/2 teaspoons marjoram
1 1/2 teaspoons savory
1/2 teaspoon ground allspice
3 cloves garlic, finely minced
2 tablespoons paprika

1. Prepare the casings. (See chapter three.)
2. Grind the meats and fat together through the coarse disk.
3. Mix the remaining ingredients with meat.
4. Stuff the casings and leave the sausage in long links. Lengths of eighteen inches to two feet are traditional.
5. Allow the sausage to dry in a cool place (under 40° F.) for three or four hours or refrigerate, uncovered, for twenty-four hours.
6. Cook by roasting in a 425° F. oven for forty-five minutes, or wrap and freeze for roasting later.

FRESH GARLIC SAUSAGE

This is very mildly seasoned and is absolutely delicious. To make four pounds:

5 feet medium hog casings
3 pounds lean pork butt, cubed
1 pound pork fat, cubed
2 teaspoons sugar
3 teaspoons finely minced garlic
1/2 teaspoon freshly fine-ground
    black pepper
1/4 cup coarse salt
1/4 teaspoon freshly grated nutmeg
1/4 teaspoon freshly grated cinnamon
1/4 teaspoon freshly ground ginger
1/4 teaspoon ground allspice
1/4 teaspoon dried thyme
1/2 cup dry white wine

1. Prepare the casings. (See chapter three.)
2. Grind the meat and fat together through the fine disk.
3. Mix the ground meat with all the remaining ingredients. Combine thoroughly.
4. Stuff the casings and twist off into four-inch links.
5. Dry, uncovered, in the refrigerator for four days, turning them often. The salt and alcohol will preserve the sausage during this period.
6. Cook by boiling in water or chicken stock, or wrap individually and freeze.

POTATIS KORV
(SWEDISH POTATO SAUSAGE)

This sausage is very popular in Sweden. For about five pounds of sausage:

4 feet medium hog casings
1 pound very lean beef from chuck,
    round or shank, cubed
1/2 pound lean pork butt, cubed
1/2 pound trimmed fat from pork
    butt, cubed
5 large potatoes
1 large onion, peeled and chopped
    coarsely
1/2 teaspoon freshly ground white
    pepper
1/2 teaspoon freshly ground black
    pepper
2 teaspoons salt
1/4 teaspoon ground allspice
1/4 teaspoon ground nutmeg
1 clove very finely minced garlic
1/4 teaspoon ground mace
Chicken broth

1. Prepare the casings. (See chapter three.)
2. Grind the meats and fat separately through the fine disk of the grinder. Refrigerate until you are ready for step five.
3. Peel and boil the potatoes in lightly salted water for ten minutes. They should be quite firm in the center. Allow them to cool before proceeding to the next step.
4. Cube the potatoes and mix together with the chopped onion. Put this mixture through the fine disk of the grinder.
5. Add the ground meats to the potatoes and onion. Add all remaining ingredients and mix well with your hands. The mixture is apt to be quite sticky so it will help if you run cold water over your hands and leave them wet for mixing.
6. Stuff the mixture into the casings either by putting it through the fine disk with the sausage stuffer attachment on the grinder or by using a separate sausage funnel.
7. Twist off into twelve-inch links. With cotton kitchen twine, tie two separate knots between each link and one knot at each end. Separate the links by cutting between the two knots between each pair of links. Bring the ends of each link together and tie to form rings.
8. Boil the rings in well-seasoned chicken broth for forty-five minutes. The sausages may be eaten warm or refrigerated and served cool.

BOUDIN BLANC

Boudin blanc is French for "white pudding," and doesn't justly describe these mild and finely textured little sausages. The recipe makes about three pounds.

4 feet medium hog casings
1/2 pound pork fat, cubed
3 large onions, peeled and sliced
1 cup milk
3/4 cup bread crumbs
1 pound veal, cubed
1 pound skinless, boneless breast of
  chicken
1/4 teaspoon nutmeg
1/4 teaspoon allspice
1/4 teaspoon fresh white pepper,
  finely ground
2 teaspoons salt
1 tablespoon parsley, chopped
1 tablespoon chives, finely chopped
2 eggs
5 egg whites
1 cup heavy cream

1. Prepare the casings. (See chapter three.)

2. Grind the pork fat through the fine disk. It will help immensely if the fat is first chilled in the freezer for about half an hour.

3. Place *half* the ground fat in a skillet and melt it down slowly over medium low heat. At no time should the pan smoke or the fat darken.

4. Add the onions to the rendered fat and cook slowly in a covered skillet for fifteen to twenty minutes, or until the onions are translucent.

5. In another pan bring the one cup of milk to a boil and add the bread crumbs. Cook, stirring constantly, until the mixture thickens enough to stick to the spoon when the spoon is inverted. Don't let the mixture burn!

6. Grind the veal and chicken together through the fine disk.

7. Combine and mix thoroughly the onions, remaining fat, veal and chicken, nutmeg, allspice, pepper, salt, parsley, and chives. Grind this mixture through the fine disk.

8. In a food processor or with an electric mixer blend the mixture until it is thoroughly mixed. Continue beating or mixing and add the whole eggs and then the egg whites. Beat a couple of minutes more and then blend in the bread crumb mixture.

9. Continue beating and add the cream, a little at a time, until it is all mixed in.

10. Stuff the mixture into the casings and twist off into four- or five-inch links. Refrigerate, covered, for one or two days.

11. Prick the casings with a needle and place them in a large pot or kettle. Cover them with a mixture of half milk and half water. Bring the liquid to a simmer and continue to simmer *very gently* for about half an hour.

12. Cool and refrigerate for up to three days. Cook by grilling or frying until just heated through.

CHAPTER FIVE

Preserving Sausage

Long before refrigeration there was the need for long-term preservation and storage of meat. Our ancient ancestors faced either feast or famine. When someone made a kill everyone feasted. Sometimes, probably more often than not, feasts were far between. Man's ingenuity eventually led him to discover various ways foodstuffs could be preserved between kills and could be easily transported and consumed when needed.

Drying is probably the oldest method of food preservation known. People learned that most of the bacteria that cause food to spoil cannot survive without water. Their life functions — like ours — depend on water.

This is good news for the home sausage maker.

Homemakers in antiquity may not have known *why* drying worked but they knew that it *did* work. Alexis Soyer, in his 1853 history of food, *The Pantropheon*, describes a recipe for an Italian sausage he calls Lucanian sausage. After instructing the cook in the proper technique of adding various ingredients such as garum, gravy, bacon, and pine nuts, he tells the maker to hang up the sausage to dry. Since the original recipe is traced by Soyer back to the Roman poet Virgil, we can rest assured that the method has stood the test of time.[1]

What is Spoilage?

Any dictionary will tell you that to "spoil" means "to become rotten, decayed or otherwise unfit for use as food." That's fine as far as it goes but it doesn't explain the process.

Spoilage is caused by the action of microorganisms on foodstuffs. Microorganisms can be divided into three groups: molds, yeasts, and bacteria.

Molds, such as the blue green growth that you find on stale bread, can harm our cured sausage (and us, in turn). Some molds

---

[1]Alexis Soyer, *The Pantropheon: or A History of Food and Its Preparation in Ancient Times*, reprint of 1853 ed., New York, 1977, p. 141.

are capable of producing a substance called mycotoxin that can make us humans extremely ill. Molds thrive on and use up the acid present in many foods, acid needed to help with food preservation.

Yeasts are probably the least dangerous of all microorganisms. This isn't to say that they are necessarily welcome guests. Yeasts can be good things: they are responsible for bread rising and grape juice turning into alcohol (and those glorious bubbles in champagne). But who wants his sausage to taste like sourdough? Yeast can lend unpleasant flavors and aromas to food, by causing food to ferment.

Bacteria are the most troublesome microorganisms with which the sausage maker has to contend. They are everywhere. But like many things in this life, the bacteria problem is double-edged. Without them life could not exist as we know it, yet if some types of bacteria were allowed to reproduce in an uncontrolled environment, human life would cease to exist.

The sausage maker, or any food processor, must be alert to avoid four causes of bacterial food poisoning: *Salmonella, Clostridium perfringens, Staphylococcus,* and *Clostridium botulinum.*

All four are found almost everywhere in the environment, and in most foods. All can cause illness, even death.

Salmonella is the most common source of food poisoning in man. These bacteria can survive in frozen and dried foods but do not reproduce at temperatures below 40° F. or above 140° F., and they will be destroyed if the food is held at above 140° F. for ten minutes.

Clostridium perfringens is extremely widespread and often strikes, causing sickness, when foods are held at improper temperatures for several hours.

Both this bacterium and *Staphylococcus aureus* are inactive at temperatures below 40° F. and above 140° F. If staph germs are allowed to multiply, they form a toxin that you cannot boil or bake away.

Clostridium botulinum organisms are the biggest villains in the microorganism arsenal. They love room temperature and moisture, and are anaerobic, which means they thrive and produce toxin in an environment that lacks oxygen. Given the proper conditions they produce spores that are so resilient they would make any science fiction writer thrilled to have thought of them before Mother Nature. These spores are harmless, but when they reproduce they give off a toxin that is so deadly that about two cups of it could kill every human being in a city the size of New York. The toxin can be destroyed by ten to twenty minutes of boiling — but whoever heard of boiled salami? More than six hours of boiling are required to kill the spores.

Fortunately we can prevent these bacteria from setting up shop in our homemade sausage.

Preventing Spoilage

As anyone who has ever put up canned foodstuffs can tell you, an ounce of prevention is worth any amount of cure.

When we were getting ready to make fresh sausage we mentioned that cleanliness is an absolute priority in sausage-making because the process and the primary ingredient — fresh meat — are tailor-made for setting up ideal conditions for contamination. If we keep in mind the following rules we can keep the problem of food spoilage to an absolute minimum.

Rule 1: Sterilize all utensils that will come in contact with the sausage as it is being prepared. These include the cutting board, knives, grinder, sausage funnel, measuring spoons, and anything else that you might use to make sausage.

Rule 2: Keep your work area clear, uncluttered, and scrupulously clean. This is a safety rule as well as a sanitation rule.

Rule 3: Wash your hands thoroughly and often. Don't wear rings. There are few kitchen chores "yukkier" than stuffing a greasy pile of meat into several yards of casing. You may not mind the feel of all that stuff on your hands (in fact if you are like me you actually enjoy it) but the bacteria don't mind it either. In fact they absolutely *thrive* at body temperature.

Rule 4: Keep meat cool at all times. Work fast, and refrigerate the meat as soon as possible. Don't leave it on the counter if you take a break.

These rules make a lot more sense if you know what prevents microbial growth. Inhibiting factors include:

1. Temperatures below 40° F. or above 140° F.
2. An acid or sugary environment
3. A lack of moisture
4. Salt
5. Alcohol

The more we tailor our sausage's environment to take into account these factors, the more certain we can be of its safety and purity.

What About Chemical Preservatives?

The next time you stop at the deli case in your local supermarket, read the labels on some of the sausages and luncheon meats. You will see such terms as BHA, BHT, sodium erythrobate, sodium or potassium nitrate, and sodium or potassium nitrite. If you were to glance through a chemical formulary at your local library you would come up with an even more extensive list. To be sure, all the ingredients on the label must meet the standards for food additives established by the Federal Food and Drug Administration (FDA) and the United States Department of Agriculture (USDA).

FDA and USDA standards are designed to prevent any harmful chemicals from coming in contact with food intended for human consumption. Recently, however, FDA licensing procedures for food additives, as well as some of the ingredients that have previously been labeled as safe, have come under increasing criticism. The saccharin and nitrate questions are notable examples.

Although this book won't condemn or defend the commercial sausage maker's use of chemical additives it will lend some perspective to the problem.

To begin with, it is impossible to cure sausage without chemical action. All the recipes in this book for cured sausage use chemicals for preservation, namely salt and alcohol. These two compounds can be just as detrimental to one's health as any concoction thought up by a chemist if they are taken in excess.

The Nitrate Problem

I wish that I could offer you a black-and-white, easy-to-understand-and-follow rule on whether to include nitrates and nitrites in cured sausages.

I can't.

Nitrates and nitrites have long been added to many meat products, including sausages, for these reasons:

1. To inhibit the growth of *clostridium botulinum*, and thus to protect the eater from botulism, as well as to lengthen the shelf-life of the meat product.

2. To make the meat a rosy red.

3. To alter the flavor.

Nitrates and nitrites have fallen into disfavor among many persons. The Food and Drug Administration explains it this way: "As with most products, nitrates and nitrites have risks as well as benefits. Under certain conditions, nitrites and amines, which are the natural breakdown products of proteins, can combine to form chemicals called nitrosamines. Experiments have shown that nitrosamines can cause cancer in animals."

The federal government has been studying this problem for more than ten years. No definite decision has been reached yet, but both the government and the industry are seeking a satisfactory substitute. The official stand, as stated by the FDA, is printed in the accompanying box.

Where does all of this leave the would-be sausage maker? I see three possibilities:

Nitrates and Nitrites:
The FDA Position

Nitrates and nitrites are added to foods to prevent botulism, a form of food poisoning which is often fatal. There have been no outbreaks of botulism that were known to be caused by processed foods that were treated with nitrates/nitrites. But a number of deaths have been caused by foods not treated with nitrates/nitrites. FDA believes it is necessary for manufacturers to use these additives to prevent the growth of poisonous substances in canned ham, bacon, and in some processed meat, poultry, and fish products.

The Risks

As with most products, nitrates and nitrites have risks as well as benefits. Under certain conditions, nitrites and amines, which are the natural breakdown products of proteins, can combine to form chemicals called nitrosamines. Experiments have shown that nitrosamines can cause cancer in animals.

There is no evidence to indicate what effects nitrosamines have in humans. We do not know, at the present time, whether the low amount of nitrates and nitrites now permitted by regulations actually combine with amines in the stomach to form nitrosamines; nor do we know to what extent nitrosamines are formed in cured meat and fish.

The U.S. Department of Agriculture (USDA) has investigated the nitrosamine content of several products. In 48 samples of processed meats, 45 showed no nitrosamines. USDA also sampled cooked sausage which had been purchased at retail stores. Of 50 samples, 3 showed trace amounts of nitrosamines; the other 47 showed no nitrosamines.

In tests by FDA, nitrosamines were found in one out of 60 hams tested. In another study, FDA found that the process of cooking bacon resulted in the formation of nitrosamines in the bacon.

The levels of nitrosamines found in these samplings were extremely low — much lower than the levels that would have to be present to cause cancer in experimental animals. However, extensive study is being conducted on the entire question of how nitrates and nitrites can be used to preserve meats and yet pose no problem for human consumption.

What is Being Done?

Based on research conducted by the meat industry in cooperation with FDA and USDA, USDA has issued proposed regulations banning all uses of sodium nitrate in meat and poultry except in dry cured and fermented sausages, and significantly reducing the levels of nitrite allowed in other cured meats.

In Summary

Nitrite is necessary to preserve ham, bacon, processed meats and some smoked fish products — and thus prevent them from causing food poisoning. In regulating the use of nitrates and nitrites, FDA must consider this benefit and weigh it against the unknown risk that these additives may help form nitrosamines which could be hazardous to health. Any change in the regulation of these additives must await results of the research now underway.

—from FDA Consumer Memo

1. Make cured sausages using the recipes that follow, and include the saltpeter (a nitrate) listed as an alternative ingredient, or substitute one of the commercial cures, following directions with it for amount.

2. Make these same sausages, but include the vitamin C listed as an alternative ingredient. As I will explain in detail, vitamin C will influence the color of the sausage but should not be counted

on to halt the growth of bacteria. This is the method I use, but I am very careful to follow the four safety rules I offered you.

3. Confine your making of sausage to the fresh varieties.

Is There an Alternative to Saltpeter?

Maybe yes. The answer is intentionally equivocal. One substance which may be added to your homemade sausage that will preserve its red color is ascorbic acid.

Ascorbic acid is available in any drugstore. Furthermore, have you ever known any one who suffered dire consequences from taking vitamin C? About one-quarter teaspoon for every five pounds of meat is sufficient and this is not, by any stretch of the imagination, an exhorbitant amount.

The jury is not yet in on the preservation action of ascorbic acid. Some sources mention it as a preservative while others say no. Don't count on it preserving your sausage. What is known is that it will hold the red color in meat. It won't have this action for as long a period as will saltpeter, but it won't cause cancer, and I can guarantee you that it won't make your sausage taste like orange juice either.

If you should decide to add ascorbic acid to your sausage — and it really can't hurt — don't crush up vitamin C tablets. They contain binders to hold everything together, and a quarter of a teaspoon of crushed tablet is not equivalent to the same measure of pure crystalline ascorbic acid. Furthermore, make certain the package label states that the ascorbic acid is U.S.P. This means it is intended for human consumption.

The Trichinosis Problem

Several cases of trichinosis are reported in the United States yearly and are largely confined to areas of the country that have large ethnic populations where people still make their own dried pork sausages. Since the meat is essentially raw even though it is dried, trichinosis is a real possibility.

Trichinosis is a disease caused by a parasitic roundworm, *Trichinella spiralis*, or, in English, trichina. The roundworm is often found in bears, pigs, and other animals of the pig family, and can infect humans if meat from an infected animal is eaten raw or untreated. It can even be transmitted by other meats, such as beef, if a contaminated knife or grinder or work area comes into contact with the infected pork. Trichinosis is nothing to fool with since its consequences can be most unpleasant and dangerous.

Trichinae mature in an infected person's intestines and most are usually killed by the body's defenses. Some, however, can survive in the form of cysts in various muscles for years.

Now that I've got you sufficiently scared let me assure you that trichinosis need not be a problem. In the case of fresh pork not used for sausage, the meat need only be cooked to an internal temperature of 137° F. Pork to be consumed raw, as in dried sausage, can be made completely safe and free of trichinae by freezing it to − 20° F. for six to twelve days, − 10° F. for ten to twenty days or 5° F. for twenty to thirty days. An accurate freezer thermometer is a must if you intend to prepare pork for dried sausage. These freezing guidelines have been set by the USDA for use by commercial packers and are perfectly safe if followed by the home sausage maker. Never taste raw pork and never sample sausage if it contains raw pork that hasn't been frozen as described.

If for some reason you can't or don't wish to tie up freezer space to treat your own sausage meat you can ask your butcher to order you some "certified" pork. Certified pork has been frozen to make it trichinosis-free and comes stamped or labeled as such. Make sure that you see the stamp or label.

Drying Equipment

If you have all the equipment necessary to make fresh sausage, you need one more thing to make dried sausage: a cold place to dry your sausage and let it hang to age for a few weeks. (You might also want to invest in a smoker but we'll get to that a bit later.) The sausage must dry for as long as a couple of months, so choose a place that will be convenient and not needed for other purposes for at least that long.

Here are a few suggestions.

The Attic

People who live in northern climates traditionally make their dried sausage in the winter.

As a boy I watched my grandfather hang up those fat links of sausage from the rafters in the attic, and dreamed of that day in early March when the first piece would be cut down and sampled. It was so cold up there you could see your breath. When I helped, my fingers would get so numb that it was a major chore to tie a simple knot in the string that held up the links. But thoughts of that first sausage, wrapped in a slab of fresh rye bread, and rich with wine and spices, made the job a lot easier.

To use your attic you must be sure of the following:

1. The temperature must remain below 40° F. for the drying time indicated in the recipes. In northern parts of the country this is a virtual certainty in winter. One or two days of premature "thaw" won't hurt but over the long haul the temperature must remain cold. The temperature in the attic shouldn't fall *below* freezing for extended periods of time either. You don't want to freeze the sausage, you want to dry it. Use an accurate thermometer to monitor the temperature.

2. Be certain that no birds or rodents can find their way into the attic. It would be very disconcerting to find a squirrel, or

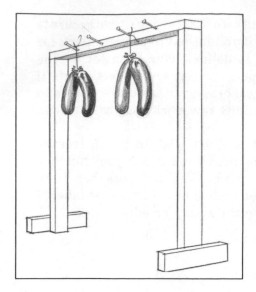

something else, swinging merrily from your drying salami. Plug any cracks or holes — even the tiniest — *before* you hang any sausage.

3. The attic should be clean. I don't mean uncluttered. Heaven knows we could open a department store with the junk that's in ours. Sweep away any dust and dirt several days before you hang up sausage. What the broom doesn't pick up will at least have a chance to settle before the sausage is hung.

4. Pound four-inch nails into a rafter. Space them about twelve inches apart and pound them in about half way. This will provide a sturdy hanger and still leave enough nail protruding to tie up the links. Choose a rafter that is at a convenient height. If the rafters are covered a simple frame made from 2 × 4s can be easily and cheaply installed.

Attics are a particularly good place to dry sausages if they have vents to provide cross ventilation and thus speed the drying process.

The Refrigerator

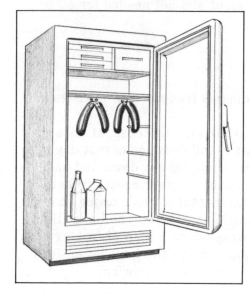

Use the refrigerator in your kitchen only as a last resort. You'll be tying up space for a fairly long time and every time you want the milk you won't want to dodge the drying salami. Besides, drying sausage gives off strong aromas, especially when still relatively fresh, and not everyone appreciates the smell of garlic and fennel at six in the morning.

If you have a second refrigerator or can obtain a used one cheaply, using it can be as practical as the attic. If you live in a warm climate, it should be your first choice.

Remove all the shelves except the top one. From this shelf you can tie the links of sausage and let them hang as you would in the attic. If you can't devote this much space to the sausage, place them on a shelf and turn them frequently to promote even drying.

Using a refrigerator can be tricky. The temperature must be adjusted to remain a fairly constant 38-40° F. Furthermore, if the refrigerator has a fan, it must be adjusted so as not to blow constantly. A constant stream of air would cause the sausage to dry on the outside before the inside had a chance to mature. Again, as with the attic method, use an accurate thermometer.

Other Solutions

If neither of the above methods is practical, use your imagination. An unheated part of the house might be a possibility. An unheated cellar might work. Be careful though: there must be some ventilation so the sausage will dry properly.

If none of these methods suits you, investigate renting space in the cooling room in a local meat locker plant. Most such plants have cooling rooms that are held at the proper temperature. This is an expensive alternative to the attic, however.

How Drying Works

In the recipes in the next chapter you will rely on three things to preserve your sausage: salt, alcohol, and temperature.

Alcohol begins the preservation process. In addition to being an excellent flavor enhancer, it has known antibacterial properties. The alcohol evaporates, however, and so by the time you eat the sausage all that will be left of the alcoholic beverage will be the taste and aroma.

Salt gets into the act long before the alcohol has evaporated. Salt draws the moisture out of the meat. Molds and bacteria have a difficult time when moisture is lacking. As the moisture is drawn out it evaporates from the meat's surface.

Temperature is almost as important as salt in preserving meat. Those little creatures that cause spoilage don't like low temperatures.

We have in effect put a triple "whammy" on any unwanted guests in our sausage. If you wish extra insurance, follow the optional directions in each recipe for adding saltpeter.

A Word about Ingredients

Everything I said in the first chapter about ingredients used in sausage applies here. And here's a word of caution: the drying process concentrates and intensifies flavors. This gives dried sausages their characteristic "spicy" reputation. Use only the purest herbs and spices, homegrown if possible, and add with a light hand.

The recipes in the next chapter call for varying amounts and kinds of alcohol, either wine or brandy or both. While it would be wasteful to use expensive wines and brandies from vintage years, it would be equally ridiculous to use the cheapest jug wine or bargain brandy. The cardinal rule in using alcohol in the preparation of food is, "If you wouldn't drink it, don't cook with it." This is all the more important when the food will be dried. The flavor — good or bad — will be intensified just as the herb and spice flavors are.

All wines and brandies contain substances known as *esters*. These are formed by the interaction of acids and alcohol and are the agents primarily responsible for the flavors and aromas in these beverages. Cheaper wines and brandies are usually harsher in their acid content and as a result the esters they contain are "rough" or, when concentrated, even unpalatable. Some inexpensive brandies even contain some pure grain alcohol. This combination makes for a very harsh tasting experience.

Shop around for wines and brandies that please both your palate and your pocketbook. If you enjoy one with a meal and can afford to put in on the table, use it in your sausage.

Smoking

Smoking cured pork sausage improves its appearance and gives it a characteristic aroma and flavor different from those of any other meat product. Careful attention must be given to prevent spoilage.

Smoking is an art, the basics of which can be taught. Like any other art, practice makes perfect and one has to learn the "feel" of the method to turn out a consistently good product.

The USDA has set forth in understandable terms the principles and procedures for smoking. The following discussion is based closely upon its guidelines.

Smokehouses

An electric home smoker like this will smoke up to forty pounds of meat at one time. Door has been removed to show interior.

The smokehouse can be simple or elaborate in design depending on the quantity of meat to be smoked. If you are a "weekend smoker" doing only a small batch of sausage now and then, an inexpensive electric smoker is most practical and economical. These smokers are readily available in most parts of the country or by mail order. They have detailed instructions to make the job easier. Check the sources of supply at the back of the book.

If you have the time, initiative, and space you might want to construct a semi-permanent or permanent smokehouse. Your structure should be of reasonably tight construction and permit easy regulation of temperature and flow of air and smoke. Special attention should be given during construction to the danger of insect and rodent infestations. Check your local building and fire codes to see if a smokehouse is allowed.

Temporary smokehouses for small quantities of meat can be

Guidelines for Smoking Sausages

1. Smoke only meat that is dry on the surface. A wet surface prevents meat from gaining a uniform smoked color.

2. Hang sausages so that they do not touch each other or the smokehouse wall. The entire surface of the meat must be exposed to ensure an even color.

3. For a fire, use hardwood such as hickory, oak, apple, cherry, pear, beech, chestnut, pecan, or maple. Fruitwoods provide a delicious flavor and aroma. Dry corncobs can be used. Never use softwoods such as pine, cedar, spruce, hemlock, fir, or cypress. They give off a sooty smoke which will give your sausage a dark, bitter taste.

constructed easily and cheaply. Construction should include a ventilated enclosure for hanging and smoking sausage as well as facilities for generating smoke and supplying it to the house. A barrel or drum with both ends removed, connected by a stovepipe or a covered trench to a fire pit can be used. Set the barrel over the upper end of the ten to twelve feet of stovepipe that slopes downward to the fire pit. Control the heat by covering the pit with sheet metal and mounding earth around the edges to cut off most of the draft. Clean muslin or burlap hung over the cleated top of the barrel will protect a one-inch opening between the barrel and the cleated top that rests on the broomsticks supporting the meat. You'll need a thermometer; a meat thermometer can be mounted to extend through a hole bored in the barrel, or it can be hung from the broomsticks.

Permanent structures suitable for smoking larger quantities of meat can be constructed from detailed plans supplied by your local extension agent. Should you decide to invest the time, energy, and money required to build a permanent smokehouse you might also look into the age-old tradition of using the buddy system. In this case, one family might have the smokehouse and allow friends and neighbors to use it. Payment is some of the smoked food.

Hot and Cold Smoking

The smoking process is either a "cold smoke" or a "hot smoke." Smoking at temperatures above 120° F. — usually about 225° F. — is called hot smoking and cooks the meat in the process. Smoking at temperatures below about 120° F. is called cold smoking and is basically a flavoring process. Hams and bacons are smoked this way. Meat that is cold smoked is essentially raw (unless it was precooked or previously preserved in some other manner) and must be treated as such. Pork, for example, would have to be frozen first, or cooked afterward, to guard against trichinosis. Cold smoked sausages should be kept refrigerated before they are cooked and eaten.

You will note that some of the following recipes call for both cold and hot smoking. The cold smoking is for flavor, the hot smoking to cook the sausage.

CHAPTER SIX

Making Cured Sausages

One of my favorite pastimes is prowling around in small ethnic grocery stores — "mom and pop stores" as they are sometimes called — because many of these places preserve the old-country tradition of making or preparing much of what they sell. One such store in my neighborhood is a favorite of mine. Walk in on a Thursday afternoon and you will find the proprietor mixing a batch of Italian sausage for the weekend trade. Hanging from a wire stretched above the meat case are dozens of links of salami and pepperoni along with balls of aged provolone cheese. Lining one of the walls are barrels of oil-cured olives and baskets of dried codfish — *baccala* — and brown paper bags of dried homemade pasta. The aromas in that little store are enough to bring on Herculean hunger pangs. The proprietor won't part with his secret recipes but he takes pride in making his sausages in full view of anyone present. It is comforting to know that not all sausage today comes packaged in plastic, having issued forth from polished chrome and stainless steel machines. Some of the best things in life are still made by hand.

Procedures and Equipment

To make the job easier follow these procedures before making any cured sausages:

1. Prepare the work area.

2. Assemble all equipment: grinder, sausage funnel, knives, mixing spoons, and a large pan for mixing. A lasagna pan is perfect.

3. Sterilize all equipment that will come in contact with the raw sausage by pouring boiling water over it.

4. Clear a space in the refrigerator large enough to accommodate the mixing pan for overnight curing.

5. Make sure the drying area is clean and ready.

6. If the recipe calls for smoking have the smokehouse or electric smoker ready. Make sure you have enough fuel on hand because once you start smoking you don't want to have to run out to scrounge up more wood chips.

Salami

Of all the various kinds of Italian dried sausages, more are labeled "salami" than anything else. The term salami encompasses many different sizes and shapes of highly spiced and salted dried sausages. Some salami is short and fat while others are quite long. Some salami has a distinct smoke flavor and in some the aroma of wine is predominant. Next time you find yourself in a real ethnic Italian market check out the varieties available. I'd be surprised if you found less than a dozen.

The term salami is the plural form of the Italian word *salame* that derives from the Latin word *sal*, meaning salt. The sausage gets its name from the ingredient that gives it much of its distinctive flavor and is primarily responsible for its preservation. Whether you prefer it sliced thin and piled high in a submarine sandwich or cured and sautéed with onions as a base for a rich tomato sauce, you will have to admit that the culinary world is a much more exciting place, thanks to salami.

GENOA SALAMI

This salami is large and robust and full of brandy.
The recipe makes ten pounds.

5 pounds lean beef from chuck, round or shank, cubed
3 pounds lean pork butt, certified or pre-frozen, cubed
2 pounds cubed pork fat
8 tablespoons coarse salt
1 cup good quality brandy
1 1/2 tablespoons sugar
2 tablespoons whole peppercorns
1 tablespoon finely ground white pepper
1 teaspoon finely ground coriander seed
2 teaspoons finely minced garlic
1 teaspoon cardamom
1/2 teaspoon ascorbic acid *or*
1 teaspoon saltpeter
4 feet large (3 1/2 - 4-inch) beef or fiber casings

1. Grind beef, pork, and fat separately through the coarse disk.
2. Mix the beef, pork, and fat together and chill in the freezer for about thirty minutes.
3. Grind the mixture through the fine disk of the grinder.
4. In a large pan mix in the remaining ingredients thoroughly.
5. Cure the mixture in the refrigerator for twenty-four hours. This is a particularly enjoyable step since every time someone opens the refrigerator the whole room will fill with the aroma of spicy salami wafting on the alcoholic wings of the brandy.
6. Prepare the casings. (See chapter three.)
7. Pack the mixture into the casings and tie off into twelve-inch links, and hang them to dry. Since the salami is a very thick sausage, eight weeks is the minimum time you should allow before sampling any. Depending upon your specific drying conditions, twelve weeks is about the optimum time required for the salami to mature and ripen into a true hard salami.

MILD SALAMI

This salami uses equal parts of pork and beef and has a milder flavor than the preceding recipe because half the alcohol in the recipe comes from white wine. Recipe is for ten pounds.

4 pounds lean beef chuck, round or shank, cubed

4 pounds lean, pre-frozen or certified pork butt, cubed

2 pounds pork fat, cubed

8 tablespoons coarse salt

1/2 cup brandy

1/2 cup dry white wine

2 tablespoons coarsely ground fresh black pepper

1 tablespoon finely ground white pepper

1 teaspoon cayenne red pepper

1 tablespoon sugar

1 teaspoon finely minced garlic

1/2 teaspoon finely ground nutmeg

1 teaspoon finely ground coriander seed

1 teaspoon finely ground fennel seed

1/2 teaspoon ascorbic acid *or*

1 teaspoon saltpeter

4 feet large (3 1/2 - 4-inch) beef or fiber casings

1. Grind beef, pork, and fat separately through the coarse disk.

2. Mix the meats and fat together, spread the mixture out on a large pan, and chill in the freezer for thirty minutes.

3. Grind the meat through the fine disk.

4. Mix in the remaining ingredients.

5. Cure the mixture in the refrigerator for twenty-four hours.

6. Prepare the casings. (See chapter three.)

7. Pack the mixture into the casings and tie off into twelve-inch links. Dry for eight to twelve weeks.

SOPPRESATTA SALAMI

This stubby sausage is sometimes called "soppresatta." I'll never forget the time I overheard someone ask for one at the deli department of a local Italian grocery store. The customer had obviously been exposed to soppresatta before but just as obviously was neither Italian nor very versed in that culture's culinary terminology. Three times he asked the girl behind the counter for one of "those supersonic sausages" before she finally guessed what it was that he wanted. Supersonic it ain't but out of this world it is! Recipe is for ten pounds:

3 pounds lean beef from chuck, round or shank, cubed

4 pounds lean, certified or pre-frozen pork butt, cubed

3 pounds cubed pork fat

8 tablespoons coarse salt

1 tablespoon finely ground fresh black pepper

2 teaspoons finely ground white pepper

1 teaspoon finely ground coriander

2 teaspoons sugar

1/2 teaspoon ascorbic acid *or*

1 teaspoon saltpeter

1 cup dry white wine

1 teaspoon finely minced garlic

4 feet large (3 1/2 - 4-inch) beef or fiber casings

1. Grind pork, beef, and fat separately through the coarse disk and then mix together in a large pan. This salami traditionally has a coarser texture than Genoa-style salami.
2. Put all the remaining ingredients except the wine and garlic into the bowl of a blender or food processor and process into a fine powder. If you don't own either of these appliances, use a mortar and pestle (which *is* the traditional method) but be prepared for a long session and sore arm muscles.
3. Add the powdered ingredients to the meat mixture, add the wine and garlic, and mix well.
4. Cure in the refrigerator for twenty-four hours.
5. Prepare the casings. (See chapter three.)
6. Stuff the mixture into the casings and tie off into six- or seven-inch links to give the soppresatta its traditional short, stubby shape.
7. Hang the sausage to dry for eight to twelve weeks.

BEER SALAMI

This salami is called "beer salami" because it is irresistible with a stein of cold lager. We're going to add a new twist to your sausage-making repertoire because this sausage uses cured instead of fresh meat. It, too, requires smoking. You could cure your own pork and corn your own beef or pick up some ham and corned beef brisket at the meat counter. For a ten pound mixture:

3 pounds corned beef brisket, cubed

7 pounds ham, fat included, cubed

1 1/2 tablespoons fresh, coarsely ground black pepper

1 tablespoon ground mace

1 1/2 tablespoons crushed mustard seed

2 teaspoons finely minced garlic

4 feet large (3 1/2 - 4-inch) beef or fiber casings

1. Grind the beef through the fine disk.
2. Mix the beef with the pork or ham cubes and mix in the seasonings.
3. Grind the mixture through the coarse disk.
4. Prepare the casings. (See chapter three.)
5. Stuff the mixture into the casings and tie off at six- or eight-inch intervals.
6. Store in the refrigerator for about twenty-four hours to mature.

7. Bring the salami to room temperature. This should take two or three hours. Wipe it dry.

8. Begin smoking the salami at about 80° F. and *gradually* raise the temperature in the smokehouse or smoker until it reaches 160° F. after four hours. Smoke an additional two hours.

9. Cool off the sausage by dunking it in a large pot of cool (not cold) water. Four or five minutes, or until it is cool to the touch, is sufficient.

10. Dry the salami thoroughly and store it in the refrigerator.

You will note that because we used cured meat in this recipe there was no need for any additional ascorbic acid, saltpeter, salt, or alcohol.

KOSHER SALAMI

This recipe makes real kosher salami if you have access to kosher-butchered beef. If not, then just like kosher dill pickles, it's the flavor that counts. Since this is an all-beef recipe, use blade cut chuck which has about the right proportions of lean to fat. Trim away all fat when cubing the meat, and thus precisely measure the amounts. Before you jump into this recipe, check on the smokehouse or dig out the instructions to the electric smoker because you'll be needing it soon. Recipe is for ten pounds.

7 1/2 pounds lean, boneless beef
   chuck, cubed
2 1/2 pounds fat from chuck, cubed
10 tablespoons salt
1 1/2 teaspoons finely minced garlic
1 tablespoon finely ground white
   pepper
1 1/2 teaspoons coarsely crushed
   white pepper
1 tablespoon crushed coriander
1 1/2 tablespoons sugar
1 cup dry white wine
1/2 teaspoon ascorbic acid *or*
1 teaspoon saltpeter
4 feet large (3 1/2 - 4-inch) beef or
   fiber casings

1. Grind the beef through the fine disk.
2. Grind the fat through the coarse disk.
3. Mix the dry ingredients with the wine and pour this mixture over the meat. Mix well.
4. Spread the mixture out on a large pan and cure in the refrigerator for at least twenty-four but preferably forty-eight hours.
5. Prepare the casings. (See chapter three.)
6. Stuff the mixture into the casings and tie off into eight- or nine-inch links.
7. Hang the sausage to dry for one week.
8. Wipe the sausage dry and smoke over a cool (about 120° F.) smoke for eight hours.
9. Increase the smoking temperature to 150°-160° F. and smoke for four additional hours.
10. Because the smoking aids in the drying process the salami should be ready to eat after about three weeks of additional drying.

GARLIC SAUSAGE

Garlic sausage is a Frenchman's steadfast friend. It is delightfully and unabashedly bourgeois, redolent with garlic and brandy. The French have a cure for the problem of garlic breath; everyone eats garlic sausage and then no one can smell the garlic on anyone else.

Garlic has been shown to have some antibiotic properties (an antibiotic is synthesized from it) and it is also a traditional remedy for high blood pressure. Shakespeare, for practical reasons no doubt, cautioned his actors against eating too much of it "to keep the breath sweet..." and Horace claimed it is more poisonous than hemlock. Back on the plus side, the Egyptian slaves wouldn't work without it and Aristophanes claimed it is an aphrodisiac. The ancient blind poet Homer credited garlic with saving Ulysses from Circe's pork barrel. You don't have to be a scholar or historian to enjoy garlic, but I thought it might make you feel better to know that you are in with some pretty famous company the next time someone winces when you open your mouth after having eaten some garlic sausage.

To make ten pounds of this potent delicacy:

6 pounds pre-frozen or certified fresh (not cured!) ham, cubed
4 pounds cubed pork fat
8 tablespoons salt
3 tablespoons finely minced garlic
1 cup brandy
1 tablespoon finely ground white pepper
1/2 teaspoon crushed bay leaf
1/2 teaspoon ground cloves
1/2 teaspoon mace
1/2 teaspoon nutmeg
1/2 teaspoon dried basil leaf
1/2 teaspoon cinnamon
1/2 teaspoon dried oregano
1/2 teaspoon sage
1/2 teaspoon thyme
1/4 teaspoon summer savory
1/4 teaspoon cayenne red pepper
1 tablespoon paprika
2 tablespoons sugar
1/2 teaspoon ascorbic acid *or*
1 teaspoon saltpeter
4 feet large (3 1/2 - 4-inch) beef or fiber casings

1. Grind the meat and fat separately through the coarse disk, mix together, and regrind through the fine disk. It will help to chill the mixture in the freezer for about thirty minutes between grindings.

2. Mix in the salt, garlic, and brandy.

3. Put all the remaining dried ingredients in a blender and process until you have a fine powder.

4. Mix the powdered herb mixture into the meat.

5. Cure the meat in the refrigerator for twenty-four hours.

6. Prepare the casings. (See chapter three.)

7. Stuff the casings and tie off into six- or seven-inch links.

8. Hang the garlic sausage to dry for about eight to twelve weeks or until sufficiently firm.

CALABRESE SALAMI

This sausage is called "calabrese" in Italian because that is where it originated. The sausage is as stark as the landscape of its birthplace. Calabria is a section of Italy that time has almost passed by. The Apennines are the central geographic feature and they dictate the manner of living in this region. Although there is some tillable land, and it does produce excellent vegetables, this region is most famous for its porkers. If there is any one region of Italy that is more proud of its sausages than any other it would probably be Calabria. You no doubt would get an argument about that statement from a Sicilian.

If there is anything that rivals the importance of pork in Calabria it is the fiery red peppers that this region seems so well suited to produce. Pork and lots of red pepper: that's Calabrese salami. For ten pounds:

7 pounds lean, cubed, pre-frozen or certified pork loin or butt

3 pounds diced pork fat

8 tablespoons coarse salt

2 teaspoons pure anise extract flavoring (or use 1/4 cup anisette)

1 tablespoon fresh, finely ground white pepper

3 tablespoons crushed red hot pepper

1/2 cup dry vermouth

1/2 cup brandy

1/2 teaspoon ascorbic acid *or*

1 teaspoon saltpeter

6 feet medium hog casings

1. Grind the lean pork through the coarse disk.
2. Grind the fat through the fine disk. Chill it in the freezer for about forty-five minutes before grinding.
3. Mix the meat and fat together and add the remaining ingredients. Mix well.
4. Prepare the casings. (See chapter three.)
5. Stuff, tie off into eight-inch links, and hang to dry for at least eight weeks before sampling.

VEAL SALAMI

This salami is different from the preceding ones in that it includes pork and veal. Even though it is still spicy enough to deserve the name salami it is sweeter than most other sausages of this type. Recipe makes ten pounds.

4 pounds lean veal cubes from butt, shoulder, or neck

3 pounds certified or pre-frozen lean pork butt, cubed

3 pounds cubed pork fat

8 tablespoons coarse salt

2 tablespoons sugar

1 tablespoon finely ground fresh black pepper

1 tablespoon finely ground white pepper

1/2 teaspoon nutmeg

1 teaspoon finely ground coriander

1 teaspoon pulverized anise seed (use a blender or mortar and pestle)

1/2 cup dry vermouth

1/2 cup brandy

1/2 teaspoon ascorbic acid *or*

1 teaspoon saltpeter

4 feet large (3 1/2 - 4-inch) beef or fiber casings

1. Grind the veal, pork, and fat through the coarse disk separately.
2. Mix the veal and fat and put this mixture through the fine disk. It will help to chill the meat and fat in the freezer for thirty minutes before the second grinding.
3. Mix the veal/fat mixture with the pork.
4. Sprinkle the remaining ingredients on the meat mixture and mix thoroughly.
5. Cure in the refrigerator for twenty-four hours.
6. Prepare the casings. (See chapter three.)
7. Stuff into the casings and tie off into six- or seven-inch links.
8. Hang the salami to dry for eight to twelve weeks.

Other Dried Sausages

The other dried sausages offer you an array of tastes, from the lingering garlic of the Italian-style dry sausage to the mild spice blended with the smoky flavor of braunschweiger.

ITALIAN-STYLE DRY SAUSAGE

The first time I had a homemade dried sausage I thought about how the flavor and scent of wine and garlic lingered on the palate long after the last morsel was eaten. To this day this recipe is one of my favorites. Some people call this sausage a salamette because the links resemble a small salami. It is simple to make and can be enjoyed about six weeks after it has been hung up to dry. For ten pounds of sausage:

8 pounds lean, cubed, certified or pre-
  frozen pork butt*
2 pounds cubed pork fat*
8 tablespoons coarse salt
1 tablespoon sugar
5 teaspoons fennel seed
2 teaspoons anise seed
1 tablespoon finely minced garlic
2 tablespoons coarse, freshly ground
  black pepper
1 tablespoon crushed red pepper
1 cup dry red wine
1/2 teaspoon ascorbic acid *or*
1 teaspoon saltpeter
6 feet medium (2-inch) hog casings

1. Grind meat and fat separately through the coarse disk.
2. Mix meat and fat together with the remaining ingredients. Use a wooden spoon or, better yet, your hands.
3. Spread the mixture in a large baking pan, cover it loosely with waxed paper, and cure it in the refrigerator for twenty-four hours.
4. Prepare casings. (See chapter three.)
5. Stuff the meat into the casings and twist off into four-inch links. Tie off each link with cotton twine.
6. Hang the links in the prepared drying area and dry for six to eight weeks. Test the sausage after six weeks by cutting off one link and slicing through it. If the texture is firm enough to suit you, the remaining sausage may be cut down and wrapped tightly for storage in the refrigerator. Prolonged drying will eventually result in a sausage that has a texture of something like beef jerky, at which time you can either gnaw on it like a dog with a bone or use it to club intruders.

---

*Prepare pork according to the instructions in chapter five to assure that it is trichinosis free.

SPANISH-STYLE CHORIZO

You're saying we made chorizos back in the section on fresh sausages and you are right. However, most chorizos are sold as dry sausages and that's what this recipe produces. It makes ten pounds of sausage.

7 pounds lean pre-frozen or certified
  pork butt, cubed
3 pounds pork fat, cubed
8 tablespoons salt
2 tablespoons finely ground, fresh
  black pepper
3 tablespoons cayenne red pepper
1 tablespoon coarsely crushed red
  pepper
2 tablespoons finely minced garlic
1 teaspoon cumin seed
1 teaspoon crushed oregano
2 tablespoons sugar
1 teaspoon fennel seed
1/4 cup red wine vinegar
3/4 cup brandy
1/2 teaspoon ascorbic acid *or*
1 teaspoon saltpeter
6 feet medium hog casings

1. Grind the meat and fat separately through the coarse disk and mix together.
2. Sprinkle the remaining ingredients on the meat and mix thoroughly.
3. Cure the sausage in the refrigerator for twenty-four hours.
4. Prepare the casings. (See chapter three.)
5. Stuff the casings and tie off into four-inch links.
6. Hang the sausage to dry for about eight weeks.

PEPPERONI

In these parts a long pepperoni sausage is called a "stick" of pepperoni and that's just about what it resembles. Most of the red color you find in commercial pepperoni is from paprika. Indeed, if it were from cayenne pepper most people would need a fire extinguisher nearby when eating it.

There are many different versions of pepperoni, some decidedly hotter than others, but most if not all rely on a pork and beef combination. All are quite pungent. Pepperoni come in different sizes, the most common being about an inch in diameter. Some commercial packers put up what they call "pizza pepperoni" which is about twice the diameter of regular pepperoni and is not as dry. This type is better able to withstand the high temperatures of a baking pizza without becoming a crispy critter. If you intend to use your pepperoni primarily as a topping for pizza, you might wish to experiment with the drying time for best results.

This makes a ten-pound batch of pepperoni.

7 pounds pre-frozen or certified pork butt, cubed, fat included

3 pounds lean beef chuck, round or shank, cubed

8 tablespoons coarse salt

1 tablespoon sugar

2 tablespoons cayenne red pepper

3 tablespoons sweet paprika*

1 tablespoon crushed anise seed

1 teaspoon garlic, very finely minced

1 cup dry red wine

1/2 teaspoon ascorbic acid *or*

1 teaspoon saltpeter

6 feet small (1/2-inch) hog, sheep or fiber casings

Cotton twine

1. Grind the pork and beef through the coarse disk separately.
2. Mix the meats together and then mix in the remaining ingredients.
3. Spread out the mixture in a large pan, cover loosely with waxed paper, and cure in the refrigerator for twenty-four hours.
4. Prepare casings. (See chapter three.)
5. Stuff the sausage into the casings and twist off into ten-inch links.
6. Using cotton twine, tie two separate knots between *every other* link, and one knot at the beginning and another at the end of the stuffed casing.
7. Cut between the double knots. This results in pairs of ten inch links. The pepperoni is hung by a string tied to the center of each pair.
8. Hang the pepperoni to dry for six to eight weeks. Once dried the pepperoni will keep, wrapped, in the refrigerator for several months.

---

*Try to find the real Hungarian paprika as it is much more flavorful.

SUMMER SAUSAGE

You don't have to wait until summer to enjoy summer sausage. Sometimes referred to as "beefstick," this sausage is sometimes made with only beef but a beef/pork combination packs more flavor. Traditionally the sausage came by its name because it was prepared in the winter to last through the summer months. This recipe requires smoking, also. It tastes great with a hunk of mozzarella or Muenster cheese on a slab of French bread washed down with a young and tender Beaujolais. Here's what you'll need for ten pounds:

6 pounds beef chuck, including about 1 pound of fat, cubed
4 pounds pre-frozen or certified pork butt, including about 1/2 pound fat, cubed
8 tablespoons coarse salt
2 tablespoons sugar
1 tablespoon finely ground white pepper
2 teaspoons crushed coriander seed
1 tablespoon whole black peppercorns
1/4 teaspoon nutmeg
1 cup red wine
1/2 teaspoon ascorbic acid *or*
1 teaspoon saltpeter
4 feet large beef or fiber casings
Flavoring solution (See step three.)

1. Grind the beef through the fine blade twice, chilling it between grindings.

2. Grind the pork through the fine blade once and mix it with the beef.

3. Make a flavoring solution with the following ingredients:

1/4 cup water
1/2 cup sugar
2 tablespoons white wine vinegar
1 tablespoon pure maple flavoring
1/2 teaspoon ground cloves
1 teaspoon pure lemon extract

Bring the water to a boil and stir in the sugar until it is dissolved. Reduce the heat so that the liquid is barely simmering and add the remaining ingredients. Turn off the flame and allow the mixture to cool.

4. Mix the flavoring solution and all remaining ingredients into the meat.

5. Cure the sausage in the refrigerator for twenty-four hours.

6. Prepare the casings. (See chapter three.)

7. Stuff the meat into the casings and tie off into six- or eight-inch links.

8. Smoke the sausage with a cool (80°-90° F.) smoke for about twelve hours.

9. Increase the smoke temperature to about 120° F. and continue to smoke for about four or five more hours or until the sausage is firm.

10. Let the sausage hang in a cool place for at least two weeks before eating.

SMOKED VENISON SAUSAGE

Venison refers to the meat of moose, elk, reindeer, and, most commonly, the white-tailed deer most people are familiar with. Venison is a dry meat and must be handled carefully to achieve satisfactory results. One small problem is that you must have a supply. If you are a hunter, this presents no obstacle. If you don't take to the fields in the fall, however, you're going to have to impose on someone who does since venison is not the most common of meats in grocery stores.

Since venison comes from wild animals, handle it with care. This means treating it as you would pork by pre-freezing it. Pork, in fact, is what we're going to use to moisten the venison enough to make our sausage palatable. The recipe makes ten pounds.

5 pounds cubed, pre-frozen venison
2 pounds lean, cubed, pre-frozen or certified pork butt
3 pounds cubed pork fat
8 tablespoons coarse salt
1 teaspoon thyme
2 teaspoons sugar
1 tablespoon fresh, finely ground black pepper
2 teaspoons finely minced garlic
1 tablespoon paprika
1 teaspoon cayenne red pepper
1 cup brandy
1/2 teaspoon ascorbic acid *or*
1 teaspoon saltpeter

A marinade consisting of the following ingredients:
1/2 cup red wine vinegar
1/2 cup red wine
2 teaspoons salt
1 small onion, sliced
1/4 cup thinly sliced carrot
1 clove garlic, finely minced
1 bay leaf
1/4 cup finely chopped heart of celery leaves (the yellow part)
1 tablespoon whole black peppercorns
6 feet medium hog casings

1. After the pre-frozen venison has thawed, prepare the marinade and pour it over the cubes of meat. Place the marinating mixture in the refrigerator for twenty-four hours.

2. Drain the venison, discard the marinade, and grind the meat through the fine disk.

3. Grind the pork and fat separately through the fine disk and mix with the venison.

4. Add the remaining ingredients and mix thoroughly. Place the sausage in the refrigerator overnight.

5. Prepare the casings. (See chapter three.)

6. Stuff the mixture into the casings and tie off into four- or five-inch links.

7. Hang the sausage to dry for forty-eight hours.

8. Cold smoke (about 70-90° F.) for about twelve hours.

9. Hang again for at least two weeks before sampling.

THURINGER SAUSAGE

This wurst *is a German invention which is more often than not marketed as a fresh sausage. It is smoked slightly and therefore will keep longer than fresh sausage but since it is not completely dried it should be consumed within a couple of weeks. This recipe is for five pounds.*

4 pounds lean cubed beef from chuck, shank or round
1 pound cubed pork fat
4 tablespoons coarse salt
1/4 teaspoon ground nutmeg
1 tablespoon finely ground white pepper
1/2 teaspoon pulverized caraway seed
1 tablespoon sugar
1/2 teaspoon crushed mustard seed
1/2 teaspoon coriander
1/2 teaspoon ground celery seed
1/2 teaspoon mace
2 teaspoons paprika
1/4 teaspoon ascorbic acid *or*
1/2 teaspoon saltpeter
4 feet medium hog casings

1. Grind the beef and pork fat separately through the fine disk and then mix them together well.
2. Mix in the remaining ingredients.
3. Cure the mixture in the refrigerator for twenty-four hours.
4. Prepare the casings. (See chapter three.)
5. Stuff the meat into the casings and twist off into four- to six-inch links. Tie off the links into pairs using two separate knots between every other link — just as we did for pepperoni. Cut the pairs apart from each other.
6. Hang to dry in a cool place or store, uncovered, in the refrigerator for two days.
7. Bring the sausage to room temperature, about four or five hours, and cold smoke (about 90° F.) for about twelve hours.
8. Hang to dry for another day or two before eating. Make sure the sausage is kept cool.

METTWURST

This delicious German sausage is smoked and precooked but, like garlic ring bologna, it must be kept refrigerated and can be stored for up to two weeks. The recipe makes five pounds of mettwurst.

3 pounds beef chuck, cubed
2 pounds pre-frozen or certified pork butt with fat, cubed
4 tablespoons coarse salt
1 teaspoon freshly ground white pepper
1/2 teaspoon ground nutmeg
1/2 teaspoon ground celery seed
1/2 teaspoon ground allspice
1/4 teaspoon freshly ground ginger root
1/4 teaspoon ground marjoram
1/4 teaspoon ascorbic acid *or*
1/2 teaspoon saltpeter
4 feet medium hog casings

1. Grind both meats through the fine disk separately and then mix them together.
2. Mix the remaining ingredients with the meat.
3. Prepare the casings. (See chapter three.)
4. Stuff the mixture into the casings and tie off into six-inch links.
5. Cure in the refrigerator for twenty-four hours.
6. Smoke at about 110-120° F. for two hours and then raise the temperature to 150° F. and smoke for two more hours.
7. Simmer in a kettle of 180-190° F. water for about thirty minutes. The sausages should rise to the top when done.
8. Place the mettwurst in a kettle of cool water for thirty minutes, remove, dry thoroughly, and refrigerate for up to two weeks.

GARLIC RING BOLOGNA

Garlic ring bologna is not really a fully cured sausage but it isn't a fresh one either. It is smoked and must be kept under refrigeration until it is eaten but it will keep for a couple of weeks. The recipe makes five pounds of this sausage.

2 pounds cubed, pre-frozen or certified pork butt
1 or 2 veal hearts (about 1 pound total)
2 pounds pork fat, cubed
5 teaspoons salt
2 teaspoons fresh, finely ground white pepper
2 teaspoons crushed mustard seed
1 teaspoon marjoram
1 teaspoon ground allspice
4 cloves garlic, very finely minced
1/4 teaspoon ascorbic acid *or*
1/2 teaspoon saltpeter
4 feet medium hog casings

1. Grind the pork, veal heart, and fat separately through the fine disk.
2. Mix the meats and fat together and sprinkle on the remaining ingredients, mixing thoroughly.
3. Chill the mixture in the refrigerator for an hour or in the freezer for half an hour and then regrind it through the fine disk.
4. Prepare the casings. (See chapter three.)
5. Stuff the casings and twist off into approximately eighteen-inch links. Be careful not to overstuff or when you try to form the links into rings they may burst. Tie double knots between the links and separate them. Bring the tied ends of each link together and tie securely, forming a ring.
6. Hang the sausage in a cool drying area or place in the refrigerator for eight to ten hours, leaving it uncovered.
7. Smoke at 110-120° F. for about two hours.
8. Bring a large pot of water to a temperature of 180-190° F. This is a bare simmer but use a thermometer to be sure.
9. Simmer the bologna rings for about twenty to thirty minutes. When done they should float to the surface.
10. Cool and store in the refrigerator for up to two weeks.

BAVARIAN SUMMER SAUSAGE

In one sense this isn't a true summer sausage because it has to be refrigerated for longer storage since it isn't as dry as most sausages that claim the name "summer sausage." In another sense, though, it is as summery a sausage as you can find because it goes beautifully with a stein of ice-cold German lager, rye bread, and a shady tree on a sultry summer afternoon. For five pounds:

4 pounds beef chuck, with fat, cubed
1 pound pre-frozen or certified pork butt, with fat, cubed
4 tablespoons coarse salt
2 tablespoons sugar
1 tablespoon whole mustard seed
2 teaspoons fresh, finely ground white pepper
1/4 teaspoon ascorbic acid *or*
1/2 teaspoon saltpeter
4 feet medium (2-inch) hog casings

1. Grind the beef and pork separately through the fine disk.
2. Mix meats together, sprinkle on the remaining ingredients, and mix well.
3. Prepare the casings. (See chapter three.)
4. Stuff the mixture into the casings and tie off into four-inch links.
5. Smoke at 140° F. for four hours or until the sausage is firm to the touch; increase the temperature to 180-190° F. and continue smoking for two hours.
6. Cool and refrigerate.

BRAUNSCHWEIGER

This German sausage is made from pure pork, is mildly spiced, and has a distinctive smoky flavor. The pork liver in the recipe lends its own special taste to the sausage. Makes five pounds.

2 1/2 pounds pre-frozen or certified pork liver, trimmed and cubed

2 1/2 pounds pre-frozen or certified pork butt with fat, cubed

1/2 cup ice water

1/4 cup nonfat dry milk

3 tablespoons coarse salt

1 tablespoon sugar

2 tablespoons finely minced onion

2 teaspoons fresh, finely ground white pepper

1 teaspoon crushed mustard seed

1/2 teaspoon ground marjoram

1/4 teaspoon ground allspice

1/4 teaspoon ascorbic acid *or*

1/2 teaspoon saltpeter

4 feet medium hog casings

1. Grind the liver and pork butt separately through the fine disk and then mix together.

2. Add the remaining ingredients, mix well, and chill in the freezer for thirty minutes. Regrind through the fine disk.

3. Prepare the casings. (See chapter three.)

4. Stuff into casings and tie off into six- or eight-inch links.

5. Simmer in a large kettle of 180-190° F. water for an hour.

6. Remove the sausage from the water, dry thoroughly, and smoke at 150° F. for two hours.

7. Place the braunschweiger in a large pot of cool water for thirty minutes, remove, dry, and store in the refrigerator for up to two weeks.

SMOKED COUNTRY-STYLE SAUSAGE

Sometimes you will see something similar to this sausage in the fresh meat case at the grocery labeled "smoked country links." It is delicious both as a breakfast sausage or as part of an hors d'oeuvres *selection. This recipe makes five pounds.*

3 pounds pre-frozen or certified pork butt, cubed

2 pounds beef chuck, about 1/4 fat, cubed

1/2 cup ice water

1/4 cup nonfat dry milk

3 tablespoons salt

1 tablespoon sugar

1 tablespoon paprika

2 teaspoons fresh, finely ground white pepper

2 teaspoons ground mustard seed

1/4 teaspoon ascorbic acid *or*

1/2 teaspoon saltpeter

4 feet small (1-inch) hog, fiber or sheep casings

1. Grind the pork through the fine disk.

2. Grind the beef through the coarse disk.

3. Mix the meats together, add remaining ingredients, and mix well.

4. Prepare the casings. (See chapter three.)

5. Stuff the meat mixture into the casings and tie off into two- to three-inch links.

6. Smoke for two hours at 180-190° F.

7. Simmer in 190° F. water for thirty minutes.

8. Remove to a kettle of cool water for half an hour, dry, and store in the refrigerator for up to two weeks.

SMOKED KIELBASA

In chapter four we made fresh Polish sausage. This smoked version is closer to what you find in the grocer's meat case. In the spring this sausage is sometimes referred to as "Easter sausage." When you see it labeled as such, saunter over to the cooler because you are also apt to find another springtime treat — bock beer. Bock beer is a traditional spring beer because in the old days brewers would clean out their vats and use the sludge at the bottom to make a dark, heavy, sweetish brew. The recipe makes five pounds.

3 pounds pre-frozen or certified pork butt, with fat, cubed

2 pounds beef chuck, trimmed and cubed

1/2 cup ice water

1/4 cup nonfat dry milk

3 tablespoons salt

1 tablespoon sugar

1 tablespoon paprika

2 teaspoons fresh, finely ground white pepper

1 tablespoon finely minced garlic

1/2 teaspoon ground marjoram

1/2 teaspoon ground thyme

1/2 teaspoon ground celery seed

1/2 teaspoon finely ground coriander

1/2 teaspoon nutmeg

1/4 teaspoon ascorbic acid *or*

1/2 teaspoon saltpeter

4 feet medium (2 1/2-inch) hog casings

1. Grind the pork through the coarse disk.
2. Grind the beef through the fine disk.
3. Mix the meats together and mix with the remaining ingredients.
4. Prepare the casings. (See chapter three.)
5. Stuff the mixture into the casings and tie off into eight- or ten-inch links.
6. Cure in the refrigerator for twenty-four hours.
7. Smoke at 180-190° F. for two hours.
8. Bring a large kettle of water to a temperature of 160-170° F. and simmer the sausage for half an hour.
9. Place the links in a kettle of cool water for half an hour, dry, and store in the refrigerator for up to two weeks.

SMOKED ITALIAN-STYLE LINKS

These sausages have a decidedly different flavor than other Italian-style sausages. This recipe yields five pounds.

3 pounds pre-frozen or certified pork butt, cubed, fat included

2 pounds beef chuck, fat included, cubed

4 tablespoons salt

3 tablespoons paprika

2 teaspoons thyme

2 teaspoons rosemary

1 teaspoon nutmeg

1/2 cup sweet vermouth

1/4 teaspoon ascorbic acid *or*

1/2 teaspoon saltpeter

4 feet medium (2-inch) hog casings

1. Grind the pork through the coarse disk.
2. Grind the beef through the fine disk.
3. Mix the meats together, sprinkle on the remaining ingredients, and mix well.
4. Prepare the casings. (See chapter three.)
5. Stuff the casings and tie off into three- or four-inch links.
6. Smoke for about two hours at 180-190° F.
7. Bring a large kettle of water to a boil, reduce heat to maintain a water temperature of 170-180° F., and simmer the sausage for thirty minutes.
8. Cool the sausage for half an hour in a pot of cool water and store under refrigeration.

CZECH YIRTRNIČKY

Italy, France, and Germany are divided into many regions within their national boundaries, and each region has contributed many unique and exciting dishes to the ethnic cuisine of its country. Many people don't know that Czechoslovakia is also divided into three distinct regions, Moravia, Bohemia, and Slovakia, each with its own distinctive cuisine. Once a part of the Austro-Hungarian Empire, the area we call Czechoslovakia is really an infant country in terms of European history. Czechoslovakia's political birthdate goes back only as far as 1918 when, as a result of the postwar turmoil, the Slovaks voted to join in union with the Czechs of Bohemia and Moravia. The union has traditionally been a very uneasy one, troubled by racial problems and the proliferation of political parties to which these problems gave rise. Czech national heritage is more a part of political compromise than national unity. Culturally Bohemia and Moravia have no more in common with Slovakia than Sicily has with Naples.

It is not necessary to understand Czech history to appreciate the country's culinary traditions any more than it is necessary to appreciate the sterling beauty of fine Bohemian crystal and lace. An appreciation of Czechoslovakia's cultural history, however, does help one understand why Czech blood sausage, liver sausage, and wine sausage (klobasy as opposed to kielbasa*) are different from their German, Austrian, and Polish counterparts.*

The recipe for yirtrničky here is Moravian, owing to my grandparents' cultural heritage. There are no doubt many other delicious versions of this sausage since many villages within the separate regions of Czechoslovakia had their own versions based upon family recipes handed down from one generation to the next. Regardless of the peculiarities of a given recipe they all rely on one basic premise: to make absolutely authentic yirtrničky you need access to a freshly butchered pig. If you raise your own hogs then you're ready to roll (or stuff, as the case may be), but if you are like most people today you are going to have to get real friendly with your butcher so you can impose upon him for some rather exotic cuts of pork. Many meat shops today get their meat shipped to them in primal cuts (loin, shoulder, etc.), neatly packaged in vacuum-packed plastic bags. It is possible that some modern meat cutters have never seen an entire freshly butchered animal carcass. Find one who still does things the old-fashioned way.

Once you've become friendly with an old-fashioned butcher, screw up your courage and with the biggest smile you can muster, ask him for a pig's head and the lungs, heart, and kidneys from a single carcass. While you are at it, also ask him for half of a freshly sliced pork liver. Contrary to what you might think he probably won't laugh at you. Instead he *will probably admire your initiative. Once your shopping cart is loaded with these exotic cuts you are ready to make a most delectable sausage. Because this recipe does not use standard, easily measurable cuts* of meat you are going to have to improvise somewhat; but bear with me: the results are worth the effort.*

1 pig's head
1 pair of lungs
1 pork heart
1 pair of pork kidneys
1/2 pork liver, freshly sliced
Stale bread
Salt
Fresh finely ground black pepper
Ground allspice
Ground cloves
Grated lemon rind
Marjoram
Several cloves of garlic, finely minced
Ascorbic acid
Hog casings, medium

I realize that so far this recipe looks like something you might expect to find in a medieval manual for prospective homemakers but it gets easier. . . .

1. In a very large kettle boil the pig's head for four or five hours or until the meat can be detached from the bone easily.

2. While the head is merrily bubbling away, in a separate kettle boil the lungs, heart, and kidneys for about two hours or until the meat is tender.

3. Chill the liver slices in the freezer for half an hour and, after cutting them into cubes, put them through the coarse disk of the meat grinder.

4. When the head and organs are cooked and cool enough to handle, scrape all the meat from the head, cube the organs, mix all with the raw liver, and put this through the fine disk.

5. Determine how much meat you have (use a measuring cup) and for each part meat combine with two parts of stale white bread that has been soaked in water and then squeezed dry.

6. Here comes the tricky part: weigh the entire mixture on a kitchen scale to determine the amount of seasonings you are going to need. If you don't have a kitchen scale, weigh yourself on the bathroom scale, weigh yourself again while you are holding the meat mixture, and subtract the first figure from the second one. Don't forget to figure in the weight of the container. (This method has obvious disadvantages if you don't want to be reminded of the fact that the bathroom scale tells you that you should be out jogging instead of making more goodies to eat.)

7. Having determined the weight of the sausage mixture, add the following ingredients in the proportions listed: 2 teaspoons salt per pound (decrease this to one teaspoon per pound if you intend to treat the sausage as fresh, using it within a week or so or freezing it), one-half teaspoon black pepper per pound, one-quarter teaspoon each of allspice, cloves, and ascorbic acid per pound and one-half teaspoon marjoram, grated lemon rind, and minced garlic per pound.

8. Prepare medium hog casings (use about one foot per pound of meat). (See chapter three.)

9. Stuff casings and tie off into six-inch links.

10. Bring a large kettle of water to a boil, reduce to a simmer,

---

*No two pigs' heads are exactly the same and neither are the internal organs, so you will have to juggle the other ingredients somewhat according to these directions.

and cook the links until they rise to the top. Don't let the water boil once the links have been added or they may burst.

11. Put sausage in a pot of cool water for a couple of minutes, remove it, and pat dry.

12. If you want fresh sausage you can refrigerate it for up to a week. It is fully cooked so it can be eaten cold. If you intend to dry it, put the links in a smoker and cold smoke it (about 120° F.) for about four hours or until it is very firm to the touch. In a cool place or in the refrigerator the sausage will now keep for months.

Congratulations! Once you've mastered the recipes in this chapter you qualify for the title *wurstmacher!*

CHAPTER SEVEN

Putting It All Together

Every summer our area becomes a showplace for ethnic cuisines. The Italians have their field (or feast) days of Saint Anthony; the Czechs, Slavs, Russians, Poles, and Greeks each have their own weekend of feasting, partying, dancing, and gaming — not to mention imbibing. For one weekend a year a public picnic area, a grassy field, or a church parking lot becomes Little Italy, Little Prague, or Little any one of many varied cultures and cuisines. The beer and wine flow freely. The music lasts until the tiny hours of the morning. Always the public is invited. And always — without exception — the charcoal fires in the makeshift brick and cinderblock pits are kept burning to accommodate the barbecued chickens, steaks, and sausages that keep the revelers reveling, holding hunger at bay and, for three days at least, making life's problems blow away on the wood-smoke-scented breeze. A soft summer's night, music, dancing, ice cold beer trickling down your throat, a hot sausage spurting juice on the first bite: it may not be heaven but it sure comes close!

Good times and good food belong to the same brotherhood. Regardless of nationality, people parade the best of their cuisine during times of partying and feasting. And one ingredient seems to play an important part in every one of them: the sausage. Sausage and good times go together like wine and cheese, like the Fourth of July and fireworks. Sausage is a fun food. I told you in the beginning of this book that sausage is fun to make and, I trust, I've convinced you of that. Now I want to show you that making sausage is not merely intrinsically satisfying but also is a very pleasant means to a most gratifying end.

The recipes in this section are family favorites. They range from the most simple and basic to extravagant, elaborate dishes suitable for dinner party extravaganzas. They all have two things in common: they all rely on some kind of sausage as an integral ingredient and they are all delicious. As I said earlier about making sausage — make these recipes your own. Try them my way first and then experiment to suit your and your family's tastes. Consider them my gift to you — your reward for becoming a *wurstmacher!*

Hors D'Oeuvres

The French call them *hors d'oeuvres*, the Italians *antipasto*, and Americans are most apt to refer to them as appetizers or munchies. In our house we call them *oover doovers*, which no doubt makes Charles de Gaulle roll over in his grave, but it nevertheless gets the message across. Next to the cracker one of the most frequently used ingredients in many before-meal treats is some kind of sausage. This attests to sausage's versatility and indicates that it can be prepared alone or in conjunction with other ingredients to make simple and quick dishes which tempt the palate without overtaxing the cook's time or energies.

BRAUNSCHWEIGER MEATBALLS

1/2 pound homemade braunschweiger sausage
2 teaspoons freshly grated onion
1/2 teaspoon minced garlic
Dash of hot pepper sauce
Salt and freshly ground black pepper to taste
2 tablespoons chopped parsley
Toothpicks

1. Mash the braunschweiger with a fork and add the onion, garlic, hot pepper sauce, salt, and pepper. Mix thoroughly.
2. Form the mixture into twenty or twenty-five little meatballs and roll each one in the parsley to coat.
3. Insert a toothpick into each ball and chill before serving. Serves 4 to 6.

BREADLESS SALAMI SANDWICH

The Earl of Sandwich would ask where the bread is in this sandwich, but since he's not around to ask just make it and enjoy it.

1/2 pound thin sliced homemade hard salami
Dijon-style mustard
Chopped parsley
Carrots cut into julienne strips
Celery cut into julienne strips

Spread each slice of salami with a thin coating of mustard, sprinkle the parsley on each slice, and place several strips of carrot and celery on each. Roll up, arrange on a platter, and serve. Serves 6 to 8 depending on how thin the salami is sliced.

BROILED SAUSAGE AND MOZZARELLA MINI-SUBMARINE SANDWICH

A whole sandwich is more than enough for a meal for one person, but if you cut it up into about eight pieces you'll have tasty appetizers.

First of all, a note about the term "submarine sandwich." It seems to depend on what part of the country you are from as to what you call a long sandwich. One common name is the "Dagwood" after the comic strip character by the same name who has been known to raid the refrigerator in the wee hours of the morning and pile almost anything high on a bun. "Grinder" is another term frequently employed and its etymology is elusive. One might guess that it derives from the fact that you really have to "grind down" to consume a sandwich of this size and scope. Another common name for a sandwich of this description is "hoagie." Your guess is as good as mine as to where that name comes from. "Hero" is another popular term and I presume that the term relates to the fact that it is a sandwich made for a hero or perhaps you might be considered a hero if you can get the whole thing down.

At any rate, one of the most common names for a long sandwich is "submarine" — no doubt because it is shaped like one. No matter where you live or what you call it, a sub is a Dagwood is a hoagie is a grinder is a hero is a sub.

1 submarine sandwich roll about twelve inches long (or use a loaf of French bread cut to size)

3/4 pound hot or sweet Italian-style sausage*

4 ounces shredded mozzarella cheese

1. Parboil the sausage over medium heat for about twenty minutes with enough water to barely cover the bottom of a skillet. Increase the heat and brown the sausage lightly, about five minutes.

2. Cut the sausage lengthwise almost but not quite all the way through and spread it out flat.

3. Cut the sub roll in the same manner as the sausage and place the sausage in the center of the roll.

4. Sprinkle the mozzarella cheese evenly over the sausage and place the sub, open side up, in a preheated broiler for two or three minutes or just until the cheese is melted. Remove from the broiler, close the sandwich, and cut into serving pieces while still warm.

Serves 8 as an appetizer.

---

*If you know you are going to be making this recipe when you are mixing up a batch of Italian-style sausage, make a link the same length as the roll you will be using and everything will fit together perfectly.

CALZONE

Calzone (pronounced căl zō′nēē) are an Italian invention which can be a main dish, a hearty snack, or delicious appetizers. As appetizers they can be quite filling so they are best served when a relatively light meal is to follow. Serve them piping hot but warn your guests to be careful not to burn their mouths on the bubbling cheese inside.

The dough for calzone is a standard Neopolitan pizza dough recipe and can be used as such.

For the dough:

1 package (1/4 ounce) dry yeast
3/4 cup plus 1/2 cup warm water
1 teaspoon salt
3 cups flour
1 tablespoon olive oil

For the filling:

1 pound bulk Italian-style sweet
   sausage
1 small onion, diced
1/2 pound pepperoni, salami, or
   soppresatta, or combination of
   these cut into 1/4-inch cubes
1 tablespoon chopped Italian parsley

Optional:

Chopped pitted black olives
Mashed anchovies
Capers
Chopped red, green and/or yellow
   peppers
Crushed red pepper

2 tablespoons melted butter
2 cups shredded mozzarella cheese
Salt and freshly ground black pepper
   to taste

1. Make the dough as follows: Mix the packet of yeast into 3/4 cup of warm water and allow to sit for fifteen minutes until bubbles form; mix salt into flour; gradually add the yeast and water and one tablespoon olive oil; work on a floured surface, gradually add the half-cup water, and knead the dough for about ten minutes. (A food processor or a large mixer with a dough hook makes child's play out of this task.) Place the dough in a lightly greased bowl, cover, put it in a warm place, and let it double in size.

2. Prepare the filling: Crumble the sausage in a skillet and sauté until it loses its pink color — five or ten minutes. Remove the sausage with a slotted spoon to a mixing bowl and add the chopped onion to the pan with the sausage drippings. Sauté the onion until it is translucent, about ten minutes. Drain the onion and add it to the sausage. Mix in the cubed sausage meat, parsley, any optional ingredients (to taste), and salt and pepper.

3. Remove the dough from the bowl and place it on a floured work surface. Divide it into four or eight equal portions. Roll each portion out into a circle so that the dough is about an eighth of an inch thick.

4. Brush each circle with melted butter, leaving a one-inch border butter-free.

5. Divide the sausage mixture equally among the circles of dough, placing it to one side of center. Sprinkle an equal amount of mozzarella on each.

6. Carefully fold each piece of dough over to form a semi-circle and press to seal the edges.

7. Brush the tops of calzone with additional melted butter or olive oil and place them on a greased cookie sheet.

8. Bake in a pre-heated 450° F. oven for about twenty-five minutes or until they are golden brown. Serve piping hot.

Serves 4 to 8.

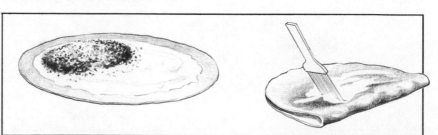

CHORIZO TOSTADAS

This recipe is a three-alarmer — or four — depending on how hot you make your chorizos. A tostada is a tortilla which is crisp-fried and covered with all sorts of yummy things.
To begin with you'll have to make some tortillas.

For tortillas:

3 cups yellow cornmeal
2 cups sifted flour
2 teaspoons salt
4 tablespoons vegetable shortening
Warm water

Topping:

1 pound fresh chorizos removed from
　the casing and crumbled
1/4 cup chopped green chili peppers
8 ounces shredded Cheddar or
　Monterey Jack cheese

1. Mix the cornmeal and salt with the flour in a bowl.
2. Cut in the shortening in small pieces with a fork as you would if you were making pie crust.
3. Begin adding water slowly, mixing it in thoroughly. You will probably need about one cup to make a workable dough.
4. Knead the dough for five minutes and then divide it into small pieces. Roll each piece into a ball. They should be about the size of a golf ball.
5. Flatten each ball and roll it out into a circle.
6. Cook each circle in an ungreased frying pan for about two minutes on each side.
7. When all the tortillas are cooked add oil to the pan and fry each tortilla until it is golden and crisp.

1. Sauté the sausage until it is lightly browned. Drain well.
2. Place an equal amount of sausage, green chilis, and cheese on each tortilla. Place them under a pre-heated broiler for a minute or two or just until the cheese melts.
Makes about 15 to 20 tostadas, enough for 8 to 10 as an appetizer.

HOT DOG WRAPAROUNDS

This is hardly a new idea as far as appetizers go but try it with your homemade wieners and see if it doesn't make a whopping difference.

1 pound homemade hot dogs
Swiss or Cheddar cheese
Bacon
Toothpicks

1. Cut the hot dogs lengthwise without cutting all the way through.
2. Cut the cheese into sticks and put one in each hot dog.
3. Wrap each hot dog with a slice of bacon and secure with a toothpick.
4. Broil until the cheese melts and the bacon is crisp. Cut into one-inch chunks and serve warm.
Serves 10-12 with about 40 pieces.

GARLIC SALAMI SQUARES

The French would call these appetizers canapés *meaning that they are a bite-sized* hors d'oeuvre *on a piece of bread.*

1/2 cup homemade garlic mayonnaise
  (*aioli*) (See step 1)
Thin sliced bread
1/2 pound homemade hard salami
3 hard-boiled eggs
1 teaspoon Pernod liqueur
Chopped parsley
Pimiento strips

1. Make the aioli as follows: mash ten cloves of garlic (peeled) with a mortar and pestle, in a food processor, or with a garlic press. In a mixing bowl scramble two egg yolks, add the garlic, salt to taste, the juice of one lemon, and a pinch of freshly ground white pepper. Mix very well. While vigorously beating with a wire whisk or with the food processor running, *slowly* dribble one and one-half cups of olive oil into the bowl. Reserve one-half cup of this aioli for the Garlic Salami Squares and refrigerate the rest (it's delicious as a dip for crisp fresh vegetables).
2. Cut off the crust from several slices of thin sliced bread (preferably French) and cut them into four squares per slice. Toast the slices until they are golden brown.
3. Cube the salami and put it through the fine disk of a meat grinder.
4. Chop the hard-boiled eggs finely and combine with the salami, Pernod, and half cup of aioli. Mix well.
5. Spread each slice of toast with some of the salami mixture, sprinkle with parsley, and criss-cross with pimiento strips. *Voila! Bon appetit!*

Makes about 24 canapés or enough for 8 to 10 servings.

LIVERWURST MUNCHIES

Liverwurst and onions. . .and mayonnaise. . .Romeo and Juliet. . .pussywillows and springtime. . .need I say more? This is a classic combination, easy to prepare and delicious.

1/2 pound homemade liverwurst
Mayonnaise
1 small Bermuda onion, sliced very
  thin
Stuffed green olives, sliced
Toasted rounds of Italian bread

1. Mash the liverwurst with just enough mayonnaise to moisten it slightly.
2. Place a thin slice of onion on each toast round. Spread liverwurst over the onion and garnish with the sliced olives.

Serves 8 to 10.

GHINA'S CHEESE AND SAUSAGE ROLL

This recipe is the creation of a dear friend, Elnora Luizzi, who, in the finest Italian tradition, keeps a warm home open to family and friends where the food, wine, and conversation flow freely. Mrs. Luizzi's grandchildren call her Ghina and since she never bothered to title this recipe I've taken the liberty of naming it for her.

Depending on the texture you like best use either the pizza dough recipe on page 62 or the pie crust dough below.

1 pound sweet Italian-style sausage, removed from casing and crumbled
1 recipe pizza or pie dough
Olive oil
8 ounces mozzarella or Swiss cheese, grated

1. Crumble the sausage in a skillet and sauté over medium heat until lightly browned, about ten minutes. Remove the meat with a slotted spoon and set aside.
2. Roll out the dough into a rectangle about twelve by eighteen inches and about a quarter of an inch thick.
3. Brush the dough with olive oil leaving a one-inch border all around.
4. Spread the sausage on the dough and top with the grated cheese.
5. Roll up the dough, jelly roll fashion, being careful to tuck in the ends and seal the edges.
6. Place the roll carefully on a greased cookie sheet, seam down, and bake in a pre-heated 375° F. oven for thirty to forty-five minutes or until the crust is crispy and golden.
7. Cool about twenty minutes and slice into half-inch thick serving pieces.
Serves 8 to 10.

OPTIONAL PIE CRUST DOUGH

2 cups sifted flour
1 teaspoon salt
2/3 cup vegetable shortening
4-6 tablespoons ice water

1. Sift the flour and salt together in a large mixing bowl.
2. Blend in the shortening, piece by piece, with a pastry blender.
3. Sprinkle the ice water on, one tablespoon at a time, mixing it well into the dough. Use only enough water to form the dough into a ball that holds together.

INSIDE-OUT SAUSAGE BALLS

Here's a new twist — the sausage is on the outside.

1/2 pound braunschweiger
Stuffed olives
Pickled cocktail onions
Chopped parsley

1. Mash the braunschweiger with a fork and then form balls around the individual olives and onions.
2. Roll each ball in chopped parsley. Chill before serving.
Serves 10-12 as an appetizer.

GUACAMOLE DIP WITH CHORIZOS

Avocados are interesting even though their flesh is rather boring to taste. In combination with other things, they take on new life. The two most interesting things you can do with an avocado are (1) grow a tree from the pit and (2) make guacamole. Whether you decide to do either or both is up to you but if you've never tried this Mexican dip I urge you to do so.

Guacamole doesn't usually have meat in it but this version is an excellent vehicle for showing off your homemade chorizos. You can tailor the recipe to either fresh or dried chorizos, depending on what you happen to have on hand.

1/2 pound fresh or dried chorizos
1 ripe avocado
1 medium tomato, cored, peeled, seeded, and finely diced
2 cloves garlic, finely minced
1/2 cup mayonnaise, preferably homemade
Dash hot pepper sauce
Salt and freshly ground black pepper

1. If you are using fresh chorizos remove them from the casing and sauté them, breaking them up with a wooden spoon until they are done, about twenty minutes. If you are using dry chorizos, cut them into half-inch cubes and put them through the fine cutting disk of your meat grinder.

2. Peel the avocado and cut it in half to remove the pit. If you plan on saving the pit to grow an avocado tree be careful not to cut through the pit's outer shell. Mash the avocado in a bowl, using the back of a fork. A food processor would simplify things here. Mash or process the avocado until you get a smooth, pureed consistency.

3. Core, peel, seed, and chop the tomato. Add it to the bowl with the avocado.

4. Mix in the chorizo, garlic, mayonnaise, hot pepper sauce, salt, and pepper. Serve chilled with corn chips.

Plenty of dip for 8-10.

MASHED POTATO SAUSAGE BALLS

The sausage is on the inside in this dish.

1 pound bulk country-style or Italian-style sweet sausage
3 cups mashed potatoes
2 eggs, well beaten
2 tablespoons water
1 cup dry breadcrumbs
2 tablespoons grated Parmesan cheese
1/2 teaspoon basil
1/2 teaspoon oregano
1 tablespoon parsley, chopped
1 teaspoon finely ground white pepper
Dash of cayenne (optional)

1. Form the sausage meat into small balls.

2. Coat each ball with mashed potatoes. This is a rather tedious procedure. It will help if the potatoes are slightly stiff.

3. Make a wash with the eggs and water.

4. Combine the bread crumbs with the remaining ingredients.

5. Dip each ball into the egg wash and then gently roll it in the seasoned bread crumbs. Place the balls on a baking sheet and let them rest for an hour or so to allow the crumb coating to set.

6. Deep fat fry the balls at about 375° F. until they are golden. Serve hot.

Serves 8-10.

PIGLETS IN A BLANKET

What looks like miniature bread loaves on the outside actually hide a real treat on the inside. If you use chorizos with this recipe you'd best play fair and warn your guests before they bite into a piglet or else have a bucket of water handy to put out the flames.

1 pound sweet or hot fresh Italian-style sausage or fresh chorizos
1 recipe pizza dough (see p. 62)

1. Parboil the sausages in just enough water to cover the bottom of the skillet until they are cooked through, about twenty-five minutes over medium heat. Drain off the liquid and brown the sausages lightly.

2. Divide the pizza dough into as many equal pieces as you have sausage links. Roll out each piece into a square.

3. Place a sausage on one end of each square and roll up the dough. Press to seal the edges.

4. Place each piglet on a greased cookie sheet and bake in a pre-heated 375° F. oven for about twenty minutes or until the dough is golden brown. Serve warm.

Makes 4-6 piglets, may serve up to 8 if piglets are sliced after cooking.

SALAMI ASPARAGUS SPEARS

This is a great way to announce the arrival of spring. Your salami has been aging all winter while your garden was asleep. When those first tender shoots of asparagus poke their heads through the chilly soil you know that spring is just around the corner.

Asparagus spears, small
1/2 pound thin sliced hard salami
Aioli (see recipe p. 64)

1. Wash and trim the asparagus under cold running water. Cut off enough of the bottom end of each spear so that all the spears are uniform in length and about as long as a slice of salami is wide. Steam until crisp-tender.

2. Spread a teaspoon of aioli on each slice of salami.

3. Place an asparagus spear on each slice and roll it up. Serve well chilled.

Serves 8-10.

PIZZA RUSTICA

Pizza rustica is in a sense a misnomer since this dish is anything but rustic. It requires careful attention to detail if you want it to be as pleasing to the eye as it is to the palate. Plan on eight servings for an antipasto or six servings as the main course at a luncheon. With a dry, well-chilled white wine and a tossed green salad this dish could be a complete meal.

1 recipe pie crust dough (see p. 65)
1/4 pound sweet Italian-style sausage, removed from the casing
2 tablespoons olive oil
1 small onion, chopped
2 cloves garlic, minced
1/4 cup (total) chopped red and green sweet peppers
1/4 cup pepperoni, diced
1/4 cup hard salami, diced
1 tablespoon chopped ripe black pitted olives
8 ounces mozzarella cheese, shredded
1/4 cup grated Parmesan cheese
1/4 cup spaghetti sauce
Salt and freshly ground black pepper

1. Prepare the pie crust dough and divide it in half. Roll out one piece and place it in a deep dish nine-inch pie plate. Roll out the other half and reserve it for the top crust.
2. Crumble the sausage in a skillet, add the olive oil, and sauté it until the meat loses its pink color, about five or ten minutes. Remove the meat with a slotted spoon and set it aside.
3. In the oil and sausage drippings sauté the onion, garlic, and chopped peppers until they are crisp-tender. Remove them with a slotted spoon. Discard the grease.
4. In a bowl mix together the sausage, pepperoni, salami, onions, peppers, and chopped olives. Add salt and pepper to taste.
5. Spread a thin layer of mozzarella on the bottom crust. Add about a third of the meat mixture and spread it evenly over the cheese. Dot with about a third of the spaghetti sauce and then sprinkle on a third of the Parmesan cheese. Repeat the layering process, ending with a layer of mozzarella cheese.
6. Place the top crust over the filling and press with a fork to seal the edges.
7. Brush the top with cold water and bake in a preheated 350° F. oven for thirty-five minutes or until the top is golden.
Serves 6-8.

SALAMI LOG

This appetizer is just the thing to impress guests with both your sausage-making abilities and with your flare for the creative.

1/2 pound thinly sliced hard salami
1 three-ounce package cream cheese at room temperature
1 teaspoon chopped fresh chives
1 teaspoon chopped fresh parsley
1 teaspoon chopped pickled capers
1 teaspoon chopped sweet gherkin

1. Spread all the slices of salami with the cream cheese.
2. Sprinkle the remaining ingredients evenly on all the slices.
3. Roll up the first slice of salami but before it is completely rolled overlap the end by about one inch on the next slice of salami and continue to roll. Repeat until you have a large roll.
4. Refrigerate for several hours to chill thoroughly and then cut into quarter-inch slices with a very sharp knife. Arrange on a platter and serve cold.
Serves 6-8.

SAUSAGE-STUFFED MUSHROOMS

This hors d'oeuvre is convenient. It looks sophisticated, as if it took a long time to prepare. A half an hour is plenty of time for anyone who knows his way around a kitchen to fix this dish and it may be refrigerated, then reheated just before guests arrive. To make this recipe work well try to find mushrooms at least an inch and a half in diameter.

18 large mushroom caps
2 tablespoons butter
1/4 pound sweet Italian- or country-
  style bulk sausage
2 tablespoons finely minced onions
2 tablespoons butter
1/4 cup dry bread crumbs
2 tablespoons dry sherry
1/2 teaspoon oregano
1 tablespoon fresh parsley, chopped
1 clove garlic, very finely minced
Salt and freshly ground black pepper
1/4 pound mozzarella cheese, grated

1. Wash the mushrooms and remove the stems. Chop the stems finely and set aside. (Some people scoff at washing mushrooms, insisting that they should only be gently wiped with a dampened paper towel. Given the fact that most of the mushrooms you buy today are grown in abandoned coal mines with plenty of horse manure, I'll wash mine, thank you. I do it quickly, so they don't absorb extra moisture.)

2. Melt two tablespoons of butter in a large skillet and gently sauté the mushroom caps for two to three minutes or until they are slightly golden, but remove before they are noticeably shrunken. Remove with a slotted spoon and drain on a paper towel.

3. Add sausage and onions to the skillet and saute for about five minutes, until the meat loses its pink color and the onions are crisp-tender. Remove with a slotted spoon.

4. Add the remaining two tablespoons of butter to the skillet along with the chopped mushroom stems and sauté another two minutes.

5. Remove from heat and add the bread crumbs, sherry, oregano, parsley, garlic, sausage and onion mixture, salt and pepper, and mix well.

6. Add the mozzarella to the mixture and stir.

7. Place an equal amount of the stuffing mixture in each cap.

8. Place the caps on a greased cookie sheet and put in a pre-heated broiler for two or three minutes or until the cheese bubbles, or refrigerate until needed.

Serves 6-8.

PUMPERNICKEL
SAUSAGE AND CHEESE SQUARES

Use any cured or dried sausage you have on hand.

1/2 pound sliced sausage, cut into one-
  inch squares
1/2 pound sliced Swiss, provolone,
  Muenster, or mozzarella cheese cut
  into one-inch squares
7 large pitted black or green stuffed
  olives, sliced
5 slices pumpernickel bread cut into
  two-inch squares

Arrange one slice of sausage, one slice of cheese and one slice of olive on each bread square. Makes about twenty servings.

Serves 8-10.

SAUSAGE-STUFFED ARTICHOKES

I've tried for many years without success to grow my own artichokes from seed. They always come up, look good for a while, and then turn their best to the sky and go to vegetable heaven. Consequently when my grocer gets in some real beauties I grab a whole bunch and rush home with them.

There are lots of things you can do with artichokes. If you're lucky enough to be able to grow your own you can let some of them mature to form large beautiful flowers. Or you can pick them when they are still young and tender (you actually eat the unopened flower bud of the plant) and boil them in salted water with some bay leaf, garlic, and lemon wedges, pull off the leaves (petals), dip them in drawn butter, and scrape off the succulent flesh between your teeth.

For variety, however, an artichoke is eminently stuffable.

4 large artichokes
4 bay leaves
4 cloves garlic, crushed
1 lemon, quartered
1 pound country-style bulk sausage or sweet Italian-style sausage removed from the casing
1/4 cup minced onion
1/4 cup Parmesan cheese
1/2 cup bread crumbs
1 egg, well beaten
1/2 cup dry white wine
1 teaspoon thyme
1 tablespoon chopped capers
Pinch of cayenne pepper
Salt and freshly ground black pepper
1/2 cup lemon juice
1/4 cup olive oil
2 cloves garlic, finely minced

1. Prepare the artichokes: Cut off the stem, leaving a flat base. Reserve the stems. Remove any bruised outer leaves. Cut about one inch off the top of each artichoke with a sharp knife. With a pair of kitchen scissors snip off the tip of each outer leaf.

2. Place the artichokes in a pot of boiling salted water along with the bay leaves, four crushed cloves of garlic, and the quartered lemon. Add the stems to the pot and cook, covered, for about half an hour. Remove from water and cool.

3. While the artichokes are bubbling, sauté the sausage in a skillet just until it loses its pink color. Remove the sausage with a slotted spoon and set it aside.

4. In the sausage drippings sauté the minced onion until it is translucent, about ten minutes.

5. In a bowl mix the sausage, onion, Parmesan cheese, bread crumbs, egg, wine, thyme, capers, cayenne, salt, pepper, and, when they are cooked, the artichoke stems, which should be chopped finely.

6. When the artichokes are cooked and cool enough to handle, pull back the leaves and remove the inner choke. (The artichoke is a member of the thistle family and if you tried to eat the choke you would see why.)

7. Fill the center of each artichoke with equal amounts of stuffing. If you have enough stuffing, place some in between the large leaves at the base.

8. Place the stuffed artichokes in a baking pan and pour the lemon juice mixed with the olive oil and minced garlic over them. Cover and bake in a pre-heated 350° F. oven for about twenty minutes or until the base leaves are very tender. Serve hot with the pan juices for dipping.

Serves 4.

SAUSAGE-STUFFED TOMATOES

Choose small (but not cherry) tomatoes for this recipe or it may be too filling for an appetizer.

8 small tomatoes
1/2 pound bulk sausage
1/4 cup chopped onion
1/4 cup chopped sweet pepper
1 clove garlic, minced
1 egg, well beaten
Dry bread crumbs
Salt and freshly ground black pepper
Butter or olive oil

1. Cut a small slice off the stem end of each tomato and remove the seeds and pulp. Be careful not to cut through the walls of the tomatoes. Sprinkle a little salt on each tomato, turn upside down on paper towels and allow to sit for about half an hour. Reserve the pulp.

2. Crumble the sausage in a skillet and sauté over medium heat until lightly browned, about ten minutes. Remove the meat with a slotted spoon and set it aside.

3. Sauté the onion, pepper, and garlic in the sausage drippings until they are crisp-tender, about five minutes. Remove them with a slotted spoon.

4. Combine the sausage, onions, peppers, and garlic with an equal amount of bread crumbs, the egg and about one-half cup of the reserved pulp. Blend the mixture thoroughly.

5. Stuff the tomatoes with the sausage mixture and place on a greased cookie sheet. Dot each tomato with the butter or olive oil. Bake in a pre-heated 400° F. oven fifteen minutes or until the tops are browned.
Serves 8.

SWEET AND SOUR SAUSAGE SPEARS

Homemade bologna, smoked kielbasa, or summer sausage is perfect in this recipe.

1/2 pound dry or semi-dry sausage cut into half-inch cubes
Pineapple cubes
Pickled beets, cubed
Toothpicks

Arrange alternating pieces of meat, pineapple, and beets on toothpicks and serve well chilled.

Note: For an interesting variation soak the skewers in slightly sweet wine or your favorite liqueur overnight.
Serves 8-10.

THURINGER SPEARS

You can use any hard or semi-hard sausage for this recipe.

1/2 pound homemade Thuringer sausage, cubed
Pickled cocktail onions
Pitted black olives
1 tablespoon olive oil
1 teaspoon liquid from the pickled onions
1/2 teaspoon sugar
Toothpicks

1. Alternate chunks of sausage with onions and olives on the toothpicks.

2. Combine the oil, pickling liquid, and sugar and mix well. Pour over spears and serve.
Serves 6-8.

SKEWERED SAUSAGE SQUARES

This is a variation on the shish kebab theme. Any hard or semi-hard homemade sausage works well in this recipe, so tailor it to what you have on hand or have a taste for.

1/2 pound cured sausage cut into half-inch cubes
1/2 pound Swiss or mozzarella cheese cut into half-inch cubes
1/2 stick butter
1 teaspoon lemon juice
1 teaspoon paprika
Dash of cayenne
Toothpicks (approximately 20)

1. Alternate cubes of sausage and cheese on the toothpicks. About two of each should do it depending on the length of your toothpicks.
2. Melt the butter in a medium-sized skillet and add the lemon juice, paprika, and cayenne.
3. Sauté the skewers gently until the cheese gets soft but does not melt. Serve warm on a heated platter.
Serves 8-10.

TOASTED SALAMI SKEWERS

4 slices thinly sliced hard salami
20 green stuffed olives
20 cocktail onions
Toothpicks
1 tablespoon olive oil
1 cup pineapple juice

1. Cut the salami into strips. You should get about five strips from each slice.
2. Assemble by pushing a toothpick through one end of a strip of salami. Skewer an olive and bring the salami strip up over the skewer to cover one side of the olive. Skewer an onion and repeat the process with the salami so that the salami forms an "S" shape around the olives and onions.
3. Combine olive oil and pineapple juice and brush on skewers.
4. Toast lightly in a pre-heated broiler for about two minutes or until warmed through.
Serves 6-8.

TEXAS-STYLE BARBECUE DOGS

Here's another elegant way to serve the lowly hot dog.

1 pound homemade hot dogs
2 tablespoons vegetable oil
1 16-ounce can tomato sauce (or use spaghetti sauce)
1 small onion, chopped
1 clove garlic, minced
1/4 cup brown sugar
1/4 cup cider vinegar
1 tablespoon Worcestershire sauce
1 teaspoon tabasco sauce
1/2 teaspoon celery seed
1/4 teaspoon fenugreek
1 teaspoon dry mustard
1 teaspoon freshly ground white pepper
1/2 teaspoon finely ground coriander
Salt to taste

1. Cut the hot dogs into one-inch pieces and sauté in the oil until browned.
2. Combine the remaining ingredients and pour over the hot dogs. Simmer gently for about ten minutes. Serve in a chafing dish with toothpicks for servers.
Serves 10-12.

SNOWBALL LIVERWURST PÂTÉ

Pâté de foie gras *is a famous (or infamous if you look at it from the goose's point of view) French* hors d'oeuvre. *In order to produce this particular delicacy the geese are put through the rather indelicate procedure of being force-fed. This operation continues, often to the point of suffocation, long enough for their livers to become enlarged. Whether you are squeamish about what they do to their geese in France or simply can't afford the high prices the gourmet merchants demand for this product, you can still eat your* pâté *and have your goose too: chicken livers and homemade liverwurst fill the bill nicely.*

4 ounces chicken livers
3 tablespoons butter
2 cloves garlic, minced
2 green onions with tops, minced
1 teaspoon basil
4 ounces liverwurst
1 tablespoon Drambuie (Scotch liqueur) or brandy
Salt and freshly ground black pepper
1 three-ounce package cream cheese
1/4 cup chopped parsley

1. Sauté the chicken livers in the butter in a skillet over medium heat for about fifteen minutes.
2. Add the garlic, onions, and basil to the skillet and sauté a moment or two longer.
3. Dice the liverwurst and add it to the livers. Remove from heat.
4. Put the mixture through a food mill to puree it.
5. Add the liqueur or brandy and salt and pepper.
6. Lightly oil a small gelatin mold (a plastic margarine cup will do very nicely) and pack the liver mixture into it firmly. Refrigerate for at least four hours.
7. Bring the cream cheese to room temperature and whip or beat it until it is smooth and creamy. (You may add an extra teaspoon of liqueur and a little finely minced garlic if you wish.)
8. Unmold the *pâté* onto a serving dish and frost it with the cream cheese.
9. Gently press the chopped parsley into the cheese frosting. Serve chilled with bread or crackers.
Serves 8-10.

Sausage Meals

One of the marvelous things about sausage is that it is so eminently adaptable. There is hardly a vegetable or fruit that doesn't go well with some kind — usually many kinds — of sausage. Part of sausage's versatility stems from the fact that it can be prepared in so many different ways. There isn't a single cuisine in the civilized world that doesn't include as part of its repertoire at least some kind of sausage.

There can be no such thing as the definitive sausage recipe book. For every idea about how to use sausage there is an infinite number of variations around that theme. You don't have to be a culinary genius to come up with some of your own variations. It helps if you like to cook but it's not necessary.

In this section we are going to treat sausage as the main ingredient in a meal. It is as easy to construct an entire meal around sausage as it is to make it in the first place.

SAUSAGE AND EGGS

COUNTRY-STYLE EGGS WITH SAUSAGE

If there is anything more versatile than sausage it would probably have to be the egg. Here's a simple recipe for one serving using both; it may be expanded for as many people as you have to serve.

1/4 pound country-style bulk sausage
2 eggs, well beaten
1 tablespoon milk
1 teaspoon freshly snipped chives
1 tablespoon grated Parmesan cheese
Salt and freshly ground black pepper

1. Sauté the sausage until it is browned, about ten minutes. Drain off most of the grease.
2. In a mixing bowl combine the eggs, milk, chives, cheese, salt and pepper. Mix well.
3. Over medium heat, pour the scrambled egg mixture into the skillet with the sausage, stirring constantly until the eggs are set.

SAUSAGE, CHICKEN LIVERS AND EGGS

Use only the freshest chicken livers in this recipe and you'll be rewarded with the most exquisite flavor.

1/2 pound bulk country, Italian, or
   chorizo sausage
1 tablespoon butter
1/2 pound fresh chicken livers, rinsed,
   dried, and coarsely chopped
1 tablespoon chopped fresh chives
8 eggs, well beaten
Salt and freshly ground black pepper

1. Sauté the sausage until it is brown, about ten minutes. Remove it with a slotted spoon and set it aside. Discard the drippings.
2. Add the butter to the skillet and sauté the chopped chicken livers four or five minutes.
3. Return the sausage to the skillet. Add the chives and the eggs, and salt and pepper to taste. Stir constantly over medium heat until the eggs are fluffy and well scrambled.
Serves 4.

SAUSAGE QUICHE

One of the best excuses I can think of for using up a few eggs is to make a quiche. A quiche is a French pie. You've no doubt heard of and probably tasted a quiche Lorraine, which is a rich concoction of custard, cheese, and bacon. This dish is a variation on the theme. My sister is fond of dividing the mixed ingredients for a quiche and making small individual servings to use as an appetizer. This recipe may certainly be adapted to that end should you so desire simply by using small tart shells instead of a pie plate. Dieters be warned: this dish is absolutely guaranteed to blow any diet — past, present or future!

Pastry:

1 cup sifted flour
1/4 teaspoon salt
1/3 cup vegetable shortening
4 tablespoons (approximately) cold
   water

1. Sift the flour together with the salt.
2. Cut the shortening into marble-sized pieces and mix it into the flour with a pastry blender.
3. Sprinkle the water on a little at a time while mixing continuously with the pastry blender. Make the dough into a ball.
4. Roll the pastry out into a circle large enough to cover an eight- or nine-inch pie plate with the edges overlapping. Line the pie plate with the pastry and trim the edges.

Filling:

1/2 pound bulk Italian-style sweet
   sausage
8 ounces fresh mushrooms, sliced
1 small onion, chopped
1/2 small sweet green pepper, cored,
   seeded, and chopped
3 eggs, well beaten
2 cups half cream and half milk
Dash of cayenne
Salt and freshly ground black pepper
4 ounces mozzarella or Gruyère
   cheese, grated
1/4 cup grated Romano cheese

1. Sauté the sausage in a skillet until it loses its pink color. Remove it with a slotted spoon and set it aside.
2. In the sausage drippings sauté the mushrooms, onions, and peppers until they are crisp-tender. Remove them with a slotted spoon and set them aside. Discard the drippings.
3. Beat the eggs, adding the half and half, cayenne, salt and pepper.
4. Put the sausage into the pastry shell. Layer the onion, mushroom, and pepper mixture evenly over the sausage. Spread the grated cheeses over all. Finally, pour the egg and cream mixture over everything.
5. Bake in a pre-heated 400° F. oven for about thirty minutes. Allow the *quiche* to cool for about ten minutes before slicing.

Note: To make individual *quiches* simply divide the pastry and ingredients between as many tart shells as you plan to use.

Serves 4 as an entree, 6-10 as an appetizer, depending on size of tart shells.

SAUSAGE AND MUSHROOM OMELET

Of all the things you can do with eggs the omelet has to be one of the most perfect. And yet many people shy away from making omelets because they think that they are difficult. Making a perfect omelet only takes a little more patience and effort than perfectly scrambling an egg. Fillings for omelets are limited only by your tastes and imagination. This is one of our favorites. The ingredients are for one serving.

1/4 pound bulk sausage (whatever kind you like)
2 tablespoons butter
1 tablespoon finely minced onion
1/4 cup chopped fresh mushrooms
2 eggs
2 tablespoons milk
Salt and freshly ground pepper

1. In a small skillet or omelet pan sauté the sausage until it is browned. Remove the sausage with a slotted spoon and discard the drippings.

2. Melt the butter in the skillet and add the onion and mushrooms. Sauté until the onions are translucent and the mushrooms have given up some of their juice.

3. While the onions and mushrooms are cooking, beat the eggs until they are smooth and frothy. Stir in the milk, salt and

4. When the onions and mushrooms are ready, pour the eggs into the pan over them. Cook the omelet over medium heat, tilting the pan and lifting the omelet's edges now and then to allow the uncooked mixture on the surface to flow underneath. When the omelet is almost set sprinkle the sausage on one side and fold the omelet over. Serve immediately. Garnish with parsley if desired.

Sausage Crepes

Crepes are fun food and yet they are very elegant. My son, Chuck, calls them "creeps," but then he hasn't discovered April in Paris yet either. Whether you have the same romantic notions about French food that I do is irrelevant: you're bound to love these sausage and crepes combinations.

Crepes are very thin pancakes. They can be made in a variety of ways and if you are lucky enough to have an electric crepe maker you're all set. A non-electric crepe pan works just as well and an ordinary skillet will even do.

BASIC ITALIAN CHEESE CREPE BATTER

1 cup all-purpose flour
1 1/2 cups milk
2 eggs
2 tablespoons Parmesan cheese
2 tablespoons Romano cheese
1 tablespoon olive oil

1. In a bowl mix all the ingredients and beat with an electric beater until the batter is smooth.

2. If you are using an electric crepe maker follow the directions that came with the appliance. Otherwise grease a crepe pan or a six-inch skillet (the non-stick variety is perfect for this) and pre-heat it for a couple of minutes.

3. Add about two tablespoons of batter to the pan and spread it to the edges. Brown one side of the crepe. The top side will be firm (not wet) to the touch when the crepe is done. Repeat until all the batter is used. Stack the cooked crepes between paper toweling or waxed paper.

BAKED ITALIAN
SAUSAGE CREPES

This recipe is very similar to an Italian dish called Baked Stuffed Manicotti which is large tubular pieces of pasta stuffed with various fillings.

1 dozen Italian cheese crepes
1 1/2 pounds sweet Italian-style
 sausage removed from the casing
1 small onion, chopped
3/4 pound fresh mushrooms, chopped
8 ounces mozzarella cheese, shredded
2 eggs, well beaten
1 egg beaten
4 cups basic tomato sauce (see p. 119)
1/4 cup grated Parmesan cheese
Salt and freshly ground black pepper
Chopped fresh parsley to garnish

1. Prepare the crepes according to the basic recipe and set aside.
2. Sauté the sausage until it is lightly browned, about ten minutes. Remove it to a mixing bowl with a slotted spoon.
3. Sauté the onions and mushrooms in the sausage drippings until the onion is translucent, about ten minutes. Remove with a slotted spoon to the bowl with the sausage.
4. Add the mozzarella and two beaten eggs to the sausage mixture and mix through well.
5. Brush each crepe with the remaining beaten egg. Divide the sausage mixture among the crepes. Place the filling on half of the crepes only and leave a one-inch border.
6. Fold the bare half of each crepe over the filling and press the edges down firmly.
7. Spread half of the tomato sauce in the bottom of a baking pan. Carefully place the crepes in a single layer on top of the sauce. Pour the rest of the sauce over the crepes and sprinkle the Parmesan cheese and parsley evenly over all.
8. Bake in a pre-heated 400° F. oven, covered, for about thirty minutes or until the sauce is bubbly and the crepes are heated through.
Serves 4.

BREAKFAST SAUSAGE
SANDWICH CREPES

This is a new way to have your pancakes and sausage for breakfast. Use the basic crepe batter recipe but leave out the grated cheese.

1 dozen crepes
1 pound country-style bulk sausage
Maple syrup

1. Prepare the crepes and keep them warm.
2. Sauté the sausage in a skillet until it is well browned. Remove it with a slotted spoon and keep it warm.
3. Layer the crepes and sausage on individual plates. (Plan on stacking at least three or four crepes per person.) Pass the maple syrup at the table.
Serves 4-6.

DAGWOOD CREPE SANDWICH

This is a knife-and-fork sandwich that can be a showcase for several of your homemade dried sausages. Dagwood Bumstead would be in heaven if he found this dish lying in wait in the back of the refrigerator at three in the morning and so would you.

1 dozen basic Italian cheese crepes (see p. 76)
1 dozen thin slices *each* of three or four different cured sausages
1 medium onion sliced thinly
1/2 cup sliced stuffed green olives
1/4 cup chopped dill pickle
1/4 cup herbed salad dressing (see recipe below)
6 slices Swiss cheese

1. Prepare the crepes.
2. Arrange half the crepes on a baking sheet. Layer half the sausages, onion, olive, and pickle on these crepes. Repeat layers with remaining crepes and ingredients.
3. Mix the herbed salad dressing as follows: to three tablespoons of red wine vinegar add 1/2 teaspoon sugar, 1/2 teaspoon salt, 1/4 teaspoon each of oregano, basil, and thyme, a dash of cayenne and freshly ground black pepper to taste. Add one tablespoon of olive oil and shake vigorously. Sprinkle an equal amount of dressing on each crepe sandwich.
4. Top each sandwich with a slice of Swiss cheese and bake in a pre-heated 400° F. oven for about ten minutes or until the cheese is melted.
Serves 6.

SALAMI CREPES

This would make a good dish to serve at a luncheon.

1 dozen Italian cheese crepes
Dijon-style mustard
1/4 pound thinly sliced homemade hard salami
1/4 pound Swiss cheese, shredded

1. Prepare the crepes.
2. Spread a thin layer of mustard on each crepe.
3. Layer equal amounts of salami and cheese on each crepe. Roll up the crepes jelly roll fashion.
4. Arrange the crepes on a cookie sheet and bake in a pre-heated 425° F. oven for about ten minutes or until the cheese is melted.
Serves 4.

SAUSAGE, ONION, AND PEPPER CREPES

Here's a classic combination in a new wrapping.

1 dozen Italian cheese crepes
3/4 pound sweet Italian-style sausage removed from the casing
1 small onion, chopped
1 small sweet green pepper, cored, seeded, and chopped

1. Prepare the crepes.
2. Sauté the sausage in a skillet until it is browned. Remove it with a slotted spoon and divide it equally among the crepes.
3. In the sausage drippings sauté the onion and pepper until they are crisp-tender, about five or ten minutes. Remove with a slotted spoon and divide among the crepes.
4. Roll up the crepes and place on a greased cookie sheet. Bake in a pre-heated 425° F. oven for about ten minutes or until warmed through.
Serves 4.

Sausage and Apples

Pork and apples are a natural go-together. The tartness of the apples contrasts with the mildness of the meat, bringing out the best in both. Any fresh pork sausages in this book can be used to advantage with apples to create a hearty and satisfying meal.

(SAUSAGE AND?) APPLE PIE

Why not? Instead of a traditional "crust" for this pie we're going to use a bed of mashed potatoes. Voila! A one-dish meal that is as satisfying as it is delicious.

1 pound fresh bulk pork sausage
1 large onion, finely chopped
1/2 cup chopped celery
2 large apples, peeled, cored, and
 thinly sliced
8 ounces coarsely chopped fresh
 mushrooms

Optional seasonings (pick and choose):
 1 teaspoon dillweed
 1/2 teaspoon marjoram
 1/2 teaspoon ground allspice
 1 teaspoon mint
 2 tablespoons parsley

1/4 cup brandy
4 tablespoons sausage drippings
4 tablespoons flour
2 cups milk
3 cups mashed potatoes
1 egg, well beaten
Salt and freshly ground black
 pepper

1. Crumble the sausage in a large skillet and lightly brown it over medium heat.

2. Add the onion, celery, apples, and mushrooms and continue cooking until all are crisp-tender.

3. Add any of the optional seasonings and brandy and cook until most of the liquid has evaporated, about 10 minutes. Remove from heat but keep warm.

4. Drain off the sausage drippings. Reserve four tablespoons. In a small saucepan heat the drippings and combine with the flour. Simmer over low heat until flour and drippings are well combined. Remove from heat and slowly add milk, stirring constantly. Cook on moderate heat, stirring constantly, until sauce thickens. Pour the sauce into the sausage mixture and stir well.

5. Prepare the mashed potatoes and stir in the egg. Salt and pepper to taste.

6. Fill a greased two-quart casserole with about half of the mashed potatoes. Spoon in the sausage mixture and top with the remaining potatoes.

7. Bake, uncovered, in a pre-heated 425° F. oven for about twenty-five minutes or until the top is well browned.

Serves 4-6.

SAUSAGE AND APPLE ROLL

This is a meat roll which bakes up just like a meatloaf.

2 pounds fresh pork sausage removed from casing if linked
3 apples, peeled, cored, and chopped
1 small onion, coarsely chopped
1 1/2 cups fresh bread crumbs
1/4 teaspoon nutmeg (optional)
1/4 teaspoon ground allspice (optional)
Dash of cayenne (optional)
Salt and freshly ground black pepper

1. On a large piece of waxed butcher paper spread out the sausage in the form of a rectangle about a half an inch thick.
2. In a mixing bowl combine the remaining ingredients.
3. Spread the apple mixture over the sausage rectangle, leaving an inch-wide border all the way around.
4. Roll up the sausage jelly roll fashion. Begin by picking up one end of the waxed paper and folding it over until the roll gets started. The meat should fall away from the paper easily. This helps prevent the sausage from breaking apart. Pinch the ends together to seal.
5. Place the roll in a greased pan and bake in a preheated 375° F. oven for one hour.
Serves 8.

SAUSAGE-STUFFED APPLES

Nothing chases away the chill of a cool, crisp autumn evening like big juicy apples begging to be stuffed and baked.

1 pound fresh bulk pork sausage
1 small onion, finely chopped
1 cup chopped celery
3-5 cups soft bread crumbs (the amount depends on how big the apples are that you are going to stuff)
1/2 cup hot water
1/2 cup dry white wine

Optional seasonings (depending on what kind of sausage you are using):
    1/2 teaspoon thyme
    1/2 teaspoon sage
    1/2 teaspoon marjoram
    1/4 teaspoon nutmeg
    1/2 teaspoon cinnamon
    1/4 teaspoon ground allspice
    Dash of cayenne
    Salt and freshly ground black pepper
6 very large baking apples (Golden Delicious, Cortland, Rome, Winesap, Northern Spy, McIntosh)

1. Brown the sausage lightly in a skillet. Remove it with a slotted spoon and set it aside.
2. In the drippings sauté the onion and celery until they are crisp-tender, about five minutes.
3. Return the sausage to the pan and add all the remaining ingredients except the apples. Mix well and remove from the heat.
4. Core the apples and peel each one about a third of the way down. Stuff the centers of the apples with equal amounts of the sausage mixture.
5. Place the stuffed apples in a greased baking pan and bake in a pre-heated 375° F. oven for forty-five minutes or until the apples are tender.
Serves 6.

SAUSAGE AND APPLE PANCAKES

Sausages and pancakes go together like bread and butter. Pancake rollups stuffed with sausage and apples with some real down-home maple syrup dribbled on top make for a super breakfast dish or a quick supper. Make your own pancakes from scratch using the recipe here or use your favorite packaged mix.

1 pound bulk country-style sausage
2 large apples, peeled, cored, and chopped coarsely
1/2 cup apple jelly
2 eggs, well beaten
1 1/2 cups milk
2 tablespoons melted butter or vegetable oil
2 cups sifted all-purpose flour
3 teaspoons baking powder
Salt to taste

1. Brown the sausage in a large skillet.
2. Add the apples and cook until tender.
3. Drain off the excess grease and stir in the apple jelly. Remove from heat and keep warm.
4. Mix together the eggs, milk, and butter or oil in a mixing bowl. Sift in the flour, baking powder, and salt. Use a whisk to beat the mixture until it is smooth and free of lumps.
5. Make the pancakes in a lightly oiled griddle. As soon as each one is done, spoon some of the sausage mixture on it, roll up, dribble on some maple syrup, and serve immediately.
Serves 4.

Sausage with Pasta, Noodles and Dumplings

Whole cuisines have been built around the noodle. The one that comes to mind first is probably the Italian. Certainly they have carried the noodle experience to its outer limits. Whether the dough is for noodles or dumplings, sausage provides a perfect counterpoint to the taste and texture. Here are some examples.

SAUSAGE AND RIGATONI

This is a classic Italian combination. In our home we enjoy it more often than our diets allow. Try it and you'll see why.

1 tablespoon olive oil
1 pound sweet Italian-style sausage links
1 small onion, peeled and chopped
1 small green pepper, seeded, cored, and chopped
4 cups tomato sauce
1 tablespoon chopped parsley
1 pound cooked rigatoni
1 12-ounce package mozzarella cheese, shredded
1/2 cup Romano cheese, grated

1. In a large skillet cook the sausages in the olive oil until they are lightly browned. Set the sausage aside to cool slightly and drain off all but two tablespoons of the drippings.
2. Sauté the onion and pepper in the remaining drippings until they are crisp-tender.
3. Add tomato sauce and parsley and simmer on medium heat.
4. Slice the sausages into one-inch pieces and add to the sauce.
5. While the sauce simmers gently, cook the rigatoni according to package directions in boiling salted water until they are *al dente* (still firm). Drain.
6. In a greased baking dish arrange layers of sauce, rigatoni, and mozzarella cheese. Sprinkle grated Romano cheese on top.
7. Bake, uncovered, in a pre-heated 425° F. oven until the sauce is bubbly and the top layer of cheese is lightly browned, about twenty minutes.
Serves 4-6.

LASAGNA WITH SAUSAGE

If there ever were a party dish for a crowd, lasagna is it. I always associate lasagna with Easter along with spit-roasted baby goat, dandelion salad, and lots of new spring wine. You don't need a special occasion to enjoy this meal, however, and neither do you need a crowd to help you polish it off. Leftover lasagna freezes very well, and if you cut it into serving portions first you can pop it out of the freezer and into the oven and there it is — an instant (almost) Italian feast.

Lasagna is a layered noodle dish and, like all generic recipes, there are many ways to make it. This recipe derives from the most traditional: plenty of meat, cheese, and rich tomato sauce.

2 tablespoons olive oil
1 pound bulk Italian sweet sausage
8 cups tomato sauce (see recipe, p. 119)
3 eggs, well beaten
1 large (46 oz.) container ricotta cheese
1/4 cup chopped parsley
Salt and freshly ground black pepper
1 pound lasagna noodles
1 twelve-ounce package mozzarella cheese
1 cup grated Parmesan cheese
1 cup grated Romano cheese

1. In a large, deep skillet or a Dutch oven heat the olive oil and brown the sausage. Pour off all but two tablespoons of the drippings.

2. Add the tomato sauce and bring to a simmer.

3. Bring a large pot of salted water to a boil.

4. In a large mixing bowl combine the eggs, ricotta cheese, parsley, salt and black pepper to taste.

5. In the pot of water, cook the lasagna noodles *al dente*, that is so that they are still slightly firm in the center. Drain thoroughly.

6. In a lasagna pan or large baking pan, spread a thin layer of the simmering tomato sauce. Add a layer of lasagna noodles. Spread some of the ricotta mixture over the noodles. Sprinkle about a quarter of the mozzarella, Parmesan, and Romano cheeses over the ricotta. Add a layer of sauce and continue layering in the same fashion until all the ingredients except the sauce are used. Reserve the leftover sauce to pass at the table. End with a layer of sauce.

7. Bake, covered, in a pre-heated 425° F. oven for thirty-five minutes or until the lasagna is bubbly. Test the center with your finger (careful! don't get burned): if it is hot to the touch the lasagna is done.

Note: Lasagna can be prepared several days in advance and stored in the refrigerator. Like a good homemade stew it improves with age.

Serving suggestion: for hearty appetites broil some Italian-style sausage links to serve with the lasagna. A tossed green salad and a *classico reserve Chianti* would make this a meal to remember.

Serves 10-12.

LASAGNA ROLLUPS
WITH SAUSAGE

My sister Renée invented lasagna rollups as an elegant but quick company dish to serve a crowd. She uses a ricotta filling (delicious!) whereas this recipe uses (how'd you guess?) your homemade Italian-style sausage.

1 1/2 pounds sweet Italian-style sausage
8 ounces mozzarella cheese, shredded
1 egg, well beaten
1 pound lasagna noodles
6 cups tomato sauce
1/2 cup grated Parmesan cheese
2 tablespoons chopped parsley
Salt and freshly ground black pepper

1. Sauté the sausage meat until it loses its pink color. Drain with a slotted spoon.

2. Mix together the sausage, mozzarella, and egg.

3. Cook the lasagna noodles according to package directions, being careful not to overcook.

4. Spread one cup of the tomato sauce evenly on the bottom of a lasagna or large baking pan.

5. Lay a lasagna noodle flat on the counter and spread some of the sausage mixture thinly on the length of the noodle. Roll the noodle jelly roll fashion. (Don't worry about the filling falling out; as it cooks it will congeal.)

6. Proceed with the rest of the noodles and filling in the same manner. Lay the rollups flat in the baking pan and pour the rest of the sauce over them.

7. Sprinkle on the Parmesan cheese and bake in a pre-heated 425° F. oven, covered, for thirty minutes or until the sauce is bubbly. Garnish with parsley and serve.

Serves 10-12.

MACARONI AND HOT DOGS

This dish isn't exactly company fare but kids love it. It is perfect for a blustery winter's evening when you don't have a lot of time to cook.

2 tablespoons oil
1 pound homemade hot dogs
1/4 cup chopped onion
2 cloves minced garlic
1 small can condensed tomato soup
1 teaspoon oregano
Salt and freshly ground black pepper
2 cups uncooked elbow or ditalini macaroni

1. Bring two quarts of water to boil for the macaroni.

2. Heat the olive oil in a large skillet and add the hot dogs, cut up into half-inch pieces, the onion, and garlic. Sauté until the hot dogs are lightly browned.

3. Add the tomato soup and half a soup can of water. Stir.

4. Add the oregano, salt and pepper.

5. Boil the macaroni until it is *al dente*. Drain and add to the sauce. Mix over medium heat until bubbly, and serve.

Serves 4-6.

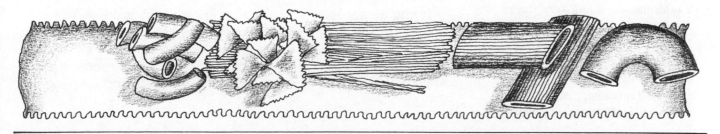

RAVIOLI WITH SAUSAGE

Here the sausage is in the sauce and serves as a flavorful counterpoint to the mildly herbed filling of the ravioli.

If you've never made your own ravioli now is the time to give it a try because it is easy to make, inexpensive, and truly delicious. You can make your own ravioli the old-fashioned way using a rolling pin, teaspoon, and knife, or you can invest about $10 in a ravioli maker. This device is well worth the money because it simplifies the job and practically guarantees success. Of course, you can always buy a package of frozen ravioli, but you'd miss half the fun of preparing this dish.

If you are going to make your own ravioli or any pasta, you should find a source of real, honest-to-goodness semolina flour. Many published recipes for homemade pasta call for all-purpose flour but for the best taste and texture, the real thing can't be beat. Semolina, the purified middlings of hard wheat, such as durum, is yellower and much coarser in texture than all-purpose flour. If you want the firmness and flavor that real Italian pasta can deliver, you should use pure semolina.

Dough:

2 1/2 cups semolina flour
1 teaspoon salt
2 eggs, well beaten
Water

Cheese filling:

1 pound ricotta cheese
1/2 pound shredded mozzarella cheese
1/2 cup grated Romano or Parmesan cheese
1/2 cup very finely chopped Italian parsley
2 eggs, well beaten
Salt and coarsely ground black pepper

Meat filling:

1/2 pound finely ground beef
1/2 pound finely ground pork
1/2 pound finely ground veal
1/4 cup grated Romano cheese
1 clove garlic, very finely minced
2 tablespoons onion, very finely minced
1/2 teaspoon basil
1/4 teaspoon nutmeg
2 eggs, well beaten
1/4 cup finely chopped parsley
Salt and freshly ground black pepper

1. Mix the semolina and salt.

2. Make a well in the center of the semolina which should be mounded on a pastry board.

3. Pour the beaten eggs into the well and mix the eggs into the flour with a fork, a little at a time.

4. Add a little water, gradually, to make the dough work up into a ball. Knead it, using additional flour if necessary, until you have a stiff but pliable ball of dough. Place the ball of dough in a bowl and cover it with a cloth until you are ready for it.

At this point you must decide whether you want a meat or cheese filling.

5. In a large mixing bowl combine all the ingredients of either the cheese or meat filling in the order they are listed and mix them with your hands.

6. Make the ravioli: If you are using a ravioli maker, roll a piece of dough about the size of a lemon out on a floured board to about the thickness of a thick knife blade (between an eighth and a sixteenth of an inch). Place this piece of dough on the serrated plate of the ravioli maker. Repeat the process with another piece of dough. Spoon about a teaspoon of filling into each indentation of the first piece of dough and place the second piece on top. With a rolling pin roll across the top sheet of dough to seal the edges and cut apart the individual ravioli.

If you do not have a ravioli maker, proceed as follows:
Roll out the first piece of dough as in the above instructions. Lay it flat on a floured board. Place about a teaspoon of filling in a grid pattern about 1 1/2 inches square. Place the second sheet of dough on top of the first and press down around the sides of

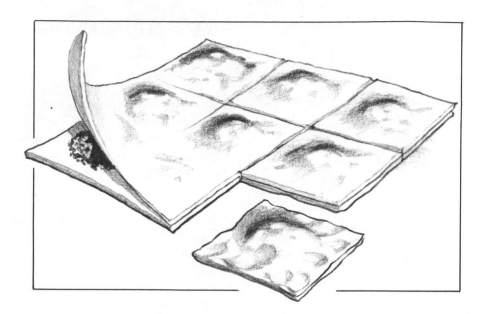

Sauce:

1 pound sweet Italian-style sausage,
    removed from the casing and
    crumbled
4 cups tomato sauce
1/2 cup grated Romano cheese
1/2 cup grated Parmesan cheese
2 tablespoons chopped parsley

each mound of filling to form squares. With a serrated edge pastry trimmer or a knife cut between the squares.

With either method, repeat the process until all the dough and filling are used. This recipe should yield about six dozen ravioli.

Set the ravioli aside on a floured surface to dry while you assemble the sauce.

7. Crumble the sausage meat in a large deep skillet and sauté it over medium heat until it is golden.

8. Add the tomato sauce and gently simmer it until it is bubbly, about twenty minutes.

9. Boil the ravioli gently in salted water for four to five minutes. Drain.

10. Layer the sauce, ravioli, and grated cheeses in individual ramekins or in a large baking dish. Bake, uncovered, in a preheated oven for about fifteen minutes or until the sauce is bubbly. Garnish with the chopped parsley and serve.

Serves 4-6.

SAUSAGE-STUFFED EGG ROLLS

Egg rolls are not pasta but the doughs and techniques of working with egg rolls are so similar I'm including this recipe in this section.

If you can obtain ready-made egg roll skins from a Chinese grocery you are all set to roll. If you are not so fortuntate, you can use my recipe for the skins.

Skins:

2/3 cup sifted all-purpose flour
1/3 cup cornstarch
1/4 teaspoon salt
1 egg
3/4 cup (approx.) water

Filling:

1/2 pound bulk fresh country-style
   sausage (or any other mildly
   flavored sausage)
1 cup very finely chopped celery
1 cup very finely shredded cabbage
1 cup finely chopped green onions
1/2 cup finely shredded carrots
1/2 cup finely chopped fresh
   mushrooms
1/4 cup finely chopped green sweet
   pepper
2 teaspoons Worcestershire sauce
1 egg
Salt and freshly ground black pepper
1 egg white

1. Sift together the flour, cornstarch, and salt.

2. Blend the egg with a quarter cup of water and gradually add it to the flour mixture. Slowly add more water and beat until the mixture is smooth.

3. Lightly oil a medium-sized skillet over medium heat. Pour about two tablespoons of the batter into the skillet and tip it in all directions to coat the bottom. If you have an electric crepe maker you can accomplish this task very easily by following the directions that came with the appliance. Cook the skins until the edges curl slightly and they are dry on top. Stack them between sheets of waxed paper until you are ready to fill them.

4. Saute the sausage in a skillet over medium heat until it is lightly browned.

5. Add all the remaining ingredients except the egg white, mix well, and sauté about two minutes to mix the flavors. Remove the mixture from the heat and allow it to cool.

6. To assemble the egg rolls, place about a quarter-cup of the filling in the center of a skin and fold two sides over to the center. Brush the two sides and the two open edges with the egg white and roll up the skin. Carefully place the egg rolls on a baking pan and refrigerate for about two hours.

7. Deep fat fry the egg rolls until they are crisp and golden. Serve with Chinese (hot) mustard.

You can make smaller versions of these egg rolls to serve as *hors d'oeuvres* by using smaller skins and less filling in each.

Serves 4.

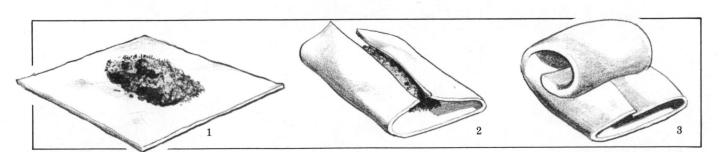

PIROGHI

Piroghi (or pirohi, or piroshki or any one of at least a half a dozen other spellings) is a Russian dish, filled dumplings made from a raised dough. Technically they aren't a pasta or noodle dish but the dough is similar so we'll include them in this section. Meatless varieties of piroghi are traditional with Russians during Lent and other varieties are common year-round. This recipe calls for a sausage filling.

Dough:

1/2 cup lukewarm water
1 (1/4 ounce) package dry yeast
2 1/2 cups sifted all-purpose flour
1 egg, well beaten
2 tablespoons rendered chicken fat or
   vegetable oil

Filling:

1 pound any variety fresh sausage
   removed from the casing
1 small onion, chopped
1 egg, well beaten

Chicken broth or water for boiling
Melted butter
Chopped parsley
Salt and freshly ground black pepper

1. Mix the yeast with one-half cup of lukewarm water and let it rest for fifteen minutes or until it becomes frothy.

2. Add the yeast to the flour with the remaining dough ingredients and mix to make a soft dough. Add a little more water if necessary.

3. Place the dough in a greased bowl and cover. Put the bowl in a warm place to allow the dough to rise. It should double in size.

4. Punch down the dough and roll it out on a floured surface until it is about an eighth of an inch thick. Cut it into circles about three inches in diameter.

5. Sauté the sausage meat until it is lightly browned. Remove it with a slotted spoon and set it aside.

6. In the sausage drippings sauté the onion until it is tender.

7. Mix the sausage, onion, and the beaten egg until thoroughly blended.

8. Place about one tablespoon of the sausage mixture on each circle of dough and fold over to form half-moons. Pinch the edges tightly to seal.

9. Place the piroghi, a few at a time, into a large pot of rapidly boiling broth or water and boil for three to four minutes. When all the piroghi are done put them in a large bowl and toss them with butter, parsley, salt and pepper, and serve warm.

Serves 4-6.

Sausage With Poultry

We've come a long way from the days of a chicken in every pot on Sunday. There was a time when poultry graced the table only when the old hen stopped laying, because it was too precious to kill and cook while it could still produce. Thank heavens those days are over.

While meat prices continue to spiral upward out of sight, poultry remains one of the biggest bargains in the meat case. Not only is it economical, but it can also be prepared in a most elegant manner. Chicken and sausage are natural go-togethers because both are so entirely versatile. Try some of the following combinations and see if you don't agree.

CHICKEN STUFFED WITH SAUSAGE
AND CZECH DRESSING

This is an excellent company dish which at first may sound rather difficult to prepare but, take my word for it, it isn't. You are either going to have to prevail upon your friendly butcher to prepare the chicken for this dish or follow the instructions here for boning out the bird. You'd best screw up your courage and prepare to carve, since very few butchers these days will take the time to bone a whole chicken without charging you an arm and a leg.

If you have never had a whole boneless chicken you are in for a treat. You might think at first that a chicken without bones can't look much like a chicken but this isn't the case at all. It not only looks like a whole roasted chicken but it carves like a roast, which means no intricate carving calisthenics at the table. All the intricacies are taken care of before the bird sees the inside of an oven.

Here's how to bone the roaster:

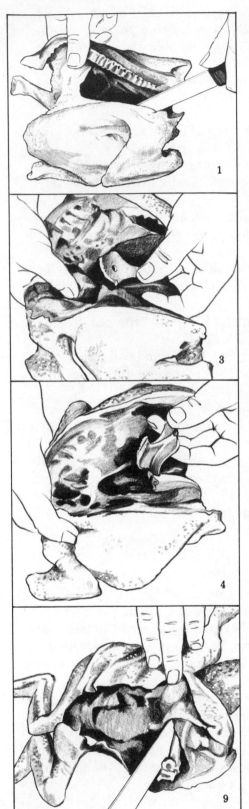

1. Place the chicken on a cutting board so that the back is facing up. Cut down the center line of the backbone from the neck to the tail. Use a sharp knife. As you work at this remember that time is not of the essence. The chicken isn't going to get up and go anywhere so take your time and you'll do a creditable job the first time.

2. With a pair of heavy-duty kitchen scissors cut out the entire backbone. Make the cut about one inch to either side of the center line. Remove the back bone, cut it in half, and reserve it along with the giblets.

3. You're now gazing into a spineless bird. You'll notice that the breastbone, that's the bone opposite from the one you just removed, runs the length of the bird until it ends up as a piece of white cartilage. Grasp both ends of the chicken and bend until the breastbone pops out and away from the cartilage.

4. Push the breast meat away from the bone until the rudder-shaped end of the bone (called the keel) is completely free of the meat.

5. With a sharp knife gently "shave" the meat away from the rib bones in one piece. Work first down one side and then the other.

6. With the ribs free split the cartilage at the front joint of the rib cage. *At all times be careful not to puncture the skin of the bird!*

7. Work the knife point into the joints where the wings are attached. Sever these joints, leaving the wings attached to the carcass by meat and skin. The wings themselves are not boned out.

8. Feel for the wishbone, make a wish, cut around it, and remove it.

9. Feel for the thigh bones (no jokes here). Cut down the center of each thigh bone until you reach the leg joint. Shave the meat away from the thigh bones, sever the joint, lift out the bones but leave the drumsticks attached just the way you did the wings. The bird is now boned. Place on a plate and refrigerate.

To prepare the dish:

1 five-pound roasting chicken, boned
1 teaspoon salt
Chicken giblets (the heart, gizzard, and liver from the roaster)
2 tablespoons olive oil
1/4 cup chopped celery
1/4 cup chopped onion
1 clove garlic, minced
1 four-five inch link Italian, Polish, country, Spanish, or other spicy sausage
2 cups, approximately, fresh bread crumbs
2 tablespoons grated carrot
1/2 cup dry white wine
1/4 teaspoon ground allspice
1/8 teaspoon rubbed sage
1/8 teaspoon crushed thyme
1 tablespoon chopped parsley
1 teaspoon Worcestershire sauce
Dash of Tabasco
Clarified butter*
2 teaspoons crushed rosemary
Salt and freshly ground black pepper

1. Place all the bones in a three-quart saucepot along with the back and giblets. Cover them with cold water, add about a teaspoon of salt, and bring to a simmer. Skim and cook for forty-five minutes.

2. Heat the oil in a large skillet and brown the sausage link. Remove the sausage and add the celery, onion, and garlic. Sauté until the vegetables are translucent, about 10 minutes.

3. Add the bread crumbs, carrot, wine, the remaining herbs except for the rosemary, and Worcestershire sauce and Tabasco. Mix well.

4. Chop the giblets into small pieces and, along with any meat you can scrape from the bones in the stock pot, add them to the skillet.

5. Remove chicken from refrigerator and place on cutting board. Spread half of stuffing mixture on the meat side of the spread-eagled bird. Don't get it too close to the edges. Place the sausage in the center. It should be almost as long as the inside of the carcass. Spread the rest of the stuffing on top of the sausage.

6. With poultry skewers and kitchen twine lace up the bird, being careful to tuck in the flaps of skin at both ends securely.

7. With a piece of twine about two feet long make a loop under each of the wings. Turn the bird over, crisscross the string and loop it under the drumsticks. Tie a secure knot. The chicken should now look more like the real thing. As it cooks, the chicken will shrink, the stuffing will expand and the bird will look perfectly true to form.

8. Place the bird on a rack in a roasting pan and insert a meat thermometer into the stuffing between the thigh and breast. Brush the bird with the clarified butter and sprinkle on the rosemary and salt and pepper to taste.

9. Roast, uncovered, in a pre-heated 375° F. oven until the thermometer reads 170° F., about 2 1/2-3 hours. Baste it frequently with clarified butter and the pan drippings as it cooks.

10. After it is removed from the oven let the chicken rest fifteen minutes before carving. Remove the wings and then slice, front to back, just as you would a roast. Each slice is framed in chicken with a perfectly round piece of sausage in the center.
Serves 8-10.

---

*Place butter in the top of a double boiler, over hot water. When it melts, the clear fat (the clarified butter) can be poured off, and the milky whey discarded or refrigerated for buttering vegetables.

CHICKEN AND
SAUSAGE CACCIATORE

Cacciatore means something fixed "in the style of the hunter." This dish need not be complicated. Elegant, yes. But to be true to its name it should be easily assembled and quickly passed from stove to table.

Adding sausage to this version serves a two-fold purpose: the dish goes further and the sausage adds a smorgasbord of interesting flavors to complement the mildly flavored chicken.

1/4 cup olive oil
1 three-pound broiler-fryer chicken
   cut into serving pieces
1 pound sweet Italian sausage links
1 medium onion, sliced very thinly
2 cloves of garlic, minced
1 medium green or yellow sweet
   pepper, sliced into quarter-inch
   strips
4 cups Italian plum tomatoes, peeled,
   cored, seeded, and chopped
2 teaspoons oregano
1 teaspoon basil
1 bay leaf
1 whole red pepper pod or one
   teaspoon crushed red pepper
Salt and freshly ground black pepper
1 pound spaghetti or spaghettini
Chopped parsley
Parmesan cheese

1. In a large skillet, brown the chicken pieces in the olive oil, about twenty minutes. Remove the chicken and keep it warm.

2. Brown the sausages in the same skillet, about twenty minutes. Remove and keep warm.

3. Discard all but two tablespoons of the accumulated drippings. Add the onion, garlic, and pepper and sauté until the onions and peppers are crisp-tender.

4. Add the chopped tomatoes, oregano, basil, bay leaf, pepper pod, and salt and pepper. Bring the sauce to a simmer and return the chicken pieces and sausages to the sauce. Simmer for thirty minutes.

5. Bring a large pot of salted water to a rapid boil for the pasta.

6. When the water is ready remove the meat from the sauce. Keep warm.

7. Cook the pasta *al dente* (slightly firm), drain and toss with butter. Place the pasta on a large platter. Arrange the meat on top of the pasta and pour the sauce over all. Sprinkle on the Parmesan cheese to taste and garnish with the chopped parsley.

   Serves 6-8.

SAUSAGE AND CHICKEN CASSEROLE

Here's another perfect marriage of chicken and sausage.

1 1/2 pounds any spicy fresh link sausage
1 three-pound broiler-fryer cut into serving pieces
1 cup flour seasoned with salt and pepper
12 small potatoes, peeled
2 cups small onions, peeled
5 carrots cut into one-inch pieces (about two cups)
1 sweet red or green pepper cut into strips
2 whole tomatoes, peeled, cored, seeded, and chopped
2 cloves garlic, minced
1 teaspoon oregano
1/2 cup dry white wine
Salt and freshly ground black pepper

1. Put enough water in a large skillet to just cover the bottom. Add the sausages and bring to a simmer. Cook until the water evaporates and the sausages give up some of their grease and begin to brown. Remove the sausages with a slotted spoon and set aside.
2. Dredge the chicken pieces in the seasoned flour. Brown them in the sausage drippings. (If the sausage was exceptionally lean, add olive oil or clarified butter to the skillet before adding the chicken).
3. Brown the potatoes with the chicken.
4. Put the meat in a casserole along with the potatoes. Add all remaining ingredients.
5. Bake, covered, in a pre-heated 375° F. oven for about sixty minutes.
Serves 4-6.

ROAST DUCKLING WITH SAUSAGE

Luganega sausage might be a good choice to use in this recipe because the lemony-orange flavors blend with the duck.

1 four-pound duckling with giblets
2 1/2 cups dry red wine
1/2 cup duck broth (from cooking the giblets)
1 small onion, chopped
2 cloves minced garlic
12 ounces chopped fresh mushrooms
Salt and freshly ground black pepper
1 pound luganega sausage

1. Wash and pat the duckling dry. Cut it into quarters. Cut off any pieces of gross fat (and save them — rendered they make excellent pastry shortening). Prick the skin in several places to allow fat to escape while cooking.
2. Place the pieces of duckling on a rack in a shallow roasting pan and bake in a pre-heated 425° F. oven, uncovered, for thirty minutes.
3. In a small saucepan cook the giblets in 3/4 cup water for thirty minutes. At the end of the cooking time there should be about a half-cup of liquid remaining.
4. Remove the duckling from the oven, drain off the accumulated drippings, remove the rack, and place the pieces of duck on the bottom of the roasting pan.
5. Combine the wine, duck broth, onion, garlic, mushrooms, salt and pepper and pour this over the duckling.
6. Reduce oven heat to 375° F. Add the sausage to the roasting pan and roast, uncovered, for about forty-five minutes. Baste the duck pieces and sausage frequently during this time.
7. Serve the pieces of duck and sausage on a platter with the wine sauce poured over them.
Serves 4-6.

CHICKEN AND
SAUSAGE PROVENÇALE

Provençale means "in the style of Provence," a geographical and political region of France. In cooking terms, provençale usually means lots of garlic, parsley, and white wine. This recipe is no exception.

2 tablespoons olive oil
1 pound fresh garlic or sweet Italian-
  style sausage links
2 tablespoons clarified butter
1 three-pound broiler-fryer chicken,
  cut into serving pieces
1/2 cup flour
3 cloves of garlic, finely minced
4 shallots, finely minced
1 cup dry white wine
1/2 cup chopped parsley
1/2 cup fine bread crumbs
Salt and freshly ground black pepper

1. Heat the olive oil in a large skillet and brown the sausages, about twenty minutes. Place the sausages on a platter and keep them warm.

2. Add the clarified butter to the oil and drippings. Dredge the chicken parts in the flour and sauté them over medium-high heat until they are golden brown, about twenty minutes. Remove the chicken from the skillet and arrange it on the platter with the sausages.

3. Drain off all but two tablespoons of the pan drippings. Add the garlic and shallots and sauté them until they are lightly golden. Be careful not to burn them because burned garlic is extremely bitter.

4. Add the wine and parsley to the skillet and reduce the liquid by half over medium high heat. Scrape the pan to get all the little brown bits clinging to the bottom.

5. Pour the juices over the chicken, coating everything evenly. Add salt and pepper to taste. Sprinkle the bread crumbs over all and place the platter in a pre-heated broiler for about ten minutes until the meat is crisp and the juices are bubbling. Use a lower rack in the broiler to assure that the meat is cooked through before it gets overdone on the outside.

Serving suggestion: a cold, dry white wine, buttered noodles or rice, and a tossed green salad go very well with this dish.

Serves 6-8.

STUFFED BREAST OF CHICKEN

Someday, I suppose, someone will catalogue everything that can be done with a breast of chicken. The French call a boneless breast of chicken a suprême *which is appropriate because some of the world's most supremely elegant dishes have been created around it. Before we get into three recipes using breasts of chicken stuffed with sausage, here are some interesting facts about* suprêmes *in general.*

First of all, don't buy boneless breasts unless you are willing to pay a premium price for them. Boning a chicken breast is simplicity in itself. If you conquered boning out an entire chicken in the recipe for Chicken Stuffed with Sausage and Czech Dressing, you can almost bone a breast with your eyes closed. Doing this yourself has the advantage of supplying you with bones and skin for your stock pot. The skin could also be rendered of its fat; the fat is excellent for cooking, and the fried skin makes delicious cracklings.

Another little fact about suprêmes: *the underside (bone side) of each breast has a little strip of flesh which runs along its length. This piece of flesh is called the fillet. It is to a chicken what a tenderloin is to a steer. And it is just as much a delicacy. Whenever you bone breasts yourself pull off this little strip (it comes off with gentle finger pressure). Freeze these fillets until you have some accumulated and then have a gourmet feast by sautéing them in a little clarified butter. Plan on at least a half a dozen per person, however, because they are very small.*

FIRST RECIPE

1 pound bulk fresh sausage (whatever you like best)

4 whole chicken breasts, boned, skinned, halved, and flattened

1 cup flour

2 eggs beaten with 2 tablespoons water

2 cups bread crumbs seasoned with the following: 1 teaspoon oregano, 1 teaspoon basil, 1 teaspoon parsley, 1 tablespoon Parmesan cheese and 1 teaspoon freshly ground white pepper

Oil for frying

1 teaspoon chopped parsley

1 lemon, quartered

1. Sauté the sausage until it is lightly browned, about ten minutes.

2. Dust each breast half with flour.

3. Place one quarter of the sausage meat on each of four of the breast halves. Leave a border all around the edges.

4. Place another breast half on top of each one with sausage. (The chicken should be moist enough to make the flour adhere at the edges).

5. Very carefully dip each combined breast into the egg wash and then coat with the seasoned bread crumbs. Press the crumbs in with the flat of your hand.

6. Heat the oil in a large skillet and sauté each breast until it is golden brown on both sides. Garnish with parsley and serve with a lemon wedge.

Serves 4.

2 whole chicken breasts, boned, skinned, and halved

1/4 pound homemade hard salami cut into quarter-inch dice

1/4 pound shredded mozzarella cheese

2 tablespoons *pignolia* (pine) nuts, lightly toasted and crushed

1 cup flour

2 eggs, beaten with 2 tablespoons water

2 cups seasoned bread crumbs (see preceding recipe)

Oil for frying

Parsley for garnish

1. With a very sharp, pointed knife cut a pocket in the plump side of each breast half. Be careful not to poke a hole through the side of the breast.

2. Mix the salami, mozzarella, and pine nuts. Divide the mixture into four equal portions and stuff the pocket of each breast.

3. Dust each breast with flour, dip in the egg wash, and coat with the seasoned bread crumbs.

4. Fry in hot oil until golden brown on each side. Garnish with parsley.

Serves 4.

THIRD RECIPE

Leave the skin on the boneless breasts for this recipe.

2 whole chicken breasts, boned, and halved

Salt and freshly ground black pepper

2 tablespoons clarified butter (see page 89)

1/4 cup minced onion

1/4 cup finely chopped mushrooms

Dash of cayenne

1 tablespoon chopped parsley

1/2 pound sweet Italian-style sausage removed from casing and crumbled

4 teaspoons grated Romano cheese

Oil for frying

4 cups tomato sauce

1/2 cup grated Parmesan cheese

1 tablespoon chopped parsley

1. Flatten each breast half and sprinkle with salt and pepper.

2. Heat the clarified butter in a skillet and sauté the onion and mushrooms until they are tender. Add a dash of cayenne and one tablespoon of parsley.

3. Mix the sautéed vegetables with the sausage meat and spread equal amounts on each breast half. Sprinkle the Romano cheese on each.

4. Roll up each breast, jelly roll fashion, and brown quickly in hot oil. The breasts should hold together as they cook but you can secure each with a toothpick to make them easier to handle.

5. Spread one cup of the tomato sauce on the bottom of a baking pan. Arrange the rollups in the pan and pour the rest of the sauce over them. Sprinkle the Parmesan cheese over them.

6. Bake, covered, in a pre-heated 425° F. oven for thirty minutes or until the breasts are tender. Garnish with parsley and serve.

Serves 4.

SAUSAGE AND CHICKEN
SAUTÉED IN RED WINE SAUCE

This dish is a variation on what is probably the most famous chicken dish in the world: coq au vin. *In keeping with the true French tradition we'll use fresh (not dried) garlic sausage.*

1/4 cup olive oil
1 three-pound broiler-fryer cut into serving pieces
1 pound fresh garlic sausage links
18 very small potatoes, peeled
1/4 cup minced celery
2 carrots, scraped and cut into one-inch pieces
1 cup baby onions
2 cloves crushed garlic
1 cup chicken stock
2 cups dry red wine
1 bay leaf
Bouquet garni (In a small square of cheesecloth put 1 teaspoon thyme leaves, 1 teaspoon marjoram, 2 sprigs of parsley, and 6 peppercorns, and tie the corners together with a string)
Salt and freshly ground black pepper

1. Heat the olive oil in the bottom of a Dutch oven and brown the chicken pieces, about twenty minutes. Remove the chicken with a slotted spoon and keep it warm.

2. Brown the sausage in the Dutch oven, about twenty minutes. Remove and keep warm.

3. Add the potatoes, celery, carrots, onions, and garlic and sauté quickly until the vegetables are browned, about ten minutes. Be careful not to burn the garlic.

4. Return the sausages and chicken to the pot. Add the chicken stock, wine, and *bouquet garni*. Bring to a simmer and cook, partially covered, for about one hour or until the chicken is tender. Remove the *bouquet garni*.

Serving suggestion: plenty of crusty French bread to sop up the juices, an endive or romaine salad, and a young Beaujolais would make this a meal to remember.

Serves 4-6.

Sausage with Other Meats

Because sausage is so versatile it can be combined with other meats, to add flavor, to add a new twist to an old recipe, or simply to stretch a dish further in an economical fashion. I'll leave to your imagination the endless possibilities but here are some of our favorites.

SAUSAGE STUFFED MEAT LOAF

Don't tell anyone that you did anything different with the meat loaf when you serve this dish for the first time and let them "ooh" and "ah" at the table when it's sliced.

2 links fresh sausage (Italian, Polish or any other spicy sausage)
1/2 pound lean ground beef
1/2 pound lean ground pork
1/2 pound ground veal
1 1/2 cups soft bread crumbs
2 eggs, well beaten
1/2 teaspoon oregano
1/2 teaspoon basil
1/4 cup finely chopped onion
1/2 teaspoon crushed mint leaves
1 clove finely minced garlic
1/8 teaspoon nutmeg
2 tablespoons chopped parsley
1/4 cup grated Romano cheese
1/2 cup dry red wine
2 shelled hard-boiled eggs
1 cup tomato sauce
1/4 cup grated Parmesan cheese

1. Parboil the sausage links in enough water to cover for fifteen minutes. Remove and drain.
2. In a large mixing bowl combine the ground meats, bread crumbs, eggs, oregano, basil, onion, mint, garlic, nutmeg, parsley, Romano cheese, and wine. Use your hands to mix well.
3. Turn half the ground meat mixture into a greased loaf pan, pressing it down firmly. Arrange the sausage links and hard-boiled eggs in the center of the meat. Press more meat in between them and then cover with the remaining meat, pressing it down firmly to seal.
4. Bake, uncovered, in a pre-heated 425° F. oven for forty-five minutes. Remove from the oven and spread the tomato sauce over the meat loaf and sprinkle on the Parmesan cheese. Return it to the oven for twenty minutes. Allow the meat loaf to stand at room temperature for about ten minutes before carving.
Serves 4.

VEAL OREGANATO WITH SAUSAGE

The basis for this dish was taught to me by my good friend, lawyer, philosopher-in-residence and all-around gourmand, Vince Luizzi. When he's not suing somebody or teaching philosophy he's apt to be puttering away in the kitchen. I've taken the liberty to change the recipe somewhat to accommodate some sweet Italian-style sausage.

1 tablespoon olive oil
8 quarter-inch thick veal cutlets cut from leg or rump
8 sweet Italian-style sausage links
4 potatoes, peeled and cut into two-inch pieces
2 sweet green peppers, cored, seeded, and cut into one-inch strips
1/2 cup chopped onion
2 cloves of garlic, finely minced
3 cups tomato sauce
1 cup dry white wine
1 1/2 teaspoon crushed oregano
1 tablespoon chopped parsley
Salt and freshly ground black pepper
1 tablespoon olive oil

1. Grease a baking pan with one tablespoon of olive oil. Spread one cup of tomato sauce evenly in the pan. Arrange the veal, sausages, potatoes, and peppers in the pan. Add the onion and garlic.
2. Pour three cups of tomato sauce over all. Add the wine.
3. Evenly sprinkle on the oregano, parsley, salt and pepper. Dribble the remaining tablespoon of olive oil over all.
4. Bake, uncovered, in a pre-heated 375° F. oven for about one hour or until the meats are tender. Place the meats and potatoes on a platter and pass the remaining sauce at the table.
Serves 6-8.

CITY CHICKEN
SAUSAGE SKEWERS

There is a dish around these parts called "city chicken." Why or how it got to be called that I don't know because it isn't even remotely related to chicken. It consists of one-inch cubes of veal and pork alternatingly skewered on wooden picks about six inches long. The skewers are floured, dipped in an egg wash, breaded, and deep fat fried.

This recipe is a variation on the city chicken theme. Substitute proportionate amounts of veal and pork cubes for the meat in this recipe if you would also like to try the original.

1/2 pound very lean finely ground bulk country sausage

1/2 pound lean ground veal seasoned with 1/4 teaspoon minced garlic, 1 teaspoon minced onion, and salt and pepper to taste

Metal or wooden skewers

1/2 cup milk

1/2 cup flour

1 egg, beaten with 2 tablespoons water

1 cup seasoned bread crumbs (see recipe p. 93)

Oil for deep frying

1. Divide the sausage and ground veal into equal portions to form one-inch meat balls.
2. String the sausage and veal balls on the skewers, alternating them until all the meat is used.
3. Dip the skewered meat in the milk, dust with flour, shaking off any excess.
4. Dip each skewer in the egg wash and then roll in the bread crumbs to coat evenly. Place the breaded skewers in the refrigerator for about thirty minutes to set the coating.
5. Heat the oil in a large skillet and fry the city chicken sausage until it's golden brown on all sides. Turn them frequently while they are cooking and don't crowd them in the pan.
6. Drain on paper towels and place them on a cookie sheet. Bake, uncovered, in a pre-heated 375° F. oven for about twenty minutes. Serve warm.

Serves 4.

HOT DOGS COOKED IN BEER

Whether hot dogs cooked in beer are better because the beer adds something intrinsic to the meat or simply because the alcoholic vapors rising from the pot whet the appetite is a matter of conjecture. Suffice it to say that they are better.

1 pound homemade hot dogs

1 12-ounce bottle of beer or ale

1 cup water

2 cups sauerkraut, rinsed and drained

1/2 teaspoon caraway seed

Hot dog buns

1. Place the hot dogs in a pot with the beer and water. Bring to a boil and then reduce heat so that the liquid barely simmers. Cook for twenty minutes.
2. Place a colander or vegetable steamer over the pan with the hot dogs and place the drained and rinsed sauerkraut in it. Sprinkle the caraway seed on the sauerkraut. The steam and vapors rising from the cooking hot dogs will heat the sauerkraut. (Cover the pot to keep the heat in.)
3. Make a bed of sauerkraut in each hot dog bun and place a dog on top. Instant picnic!

Serves 4.

DOUBLE THICK PORK CHOPS STUFFED WITH SAUSAGE

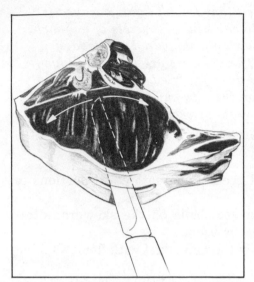

There is only one way to stuff a pork chop so that the stuffing stays put. It's surprising how many people don't know how to do it.

The most common method of stuffing a pork chop is to slit it end to end opposite the bone. This is commonly called butterflying because that's what it resembles. When the stuffing is placed in the center and the chop is skewered shut and baked, however, the chop shrinks and the filling leaks out.

For a much neater stuffed pork chop try this: with a very sharp pointed paring knife pierce the chop in the center of the edge opposite the bone, then thrust the knife all the way to the bone, as if you were going to make two pork chops out of it. Without making that opening any larger, work a pocket into the chop by moving the knife first in one direction, and then, turning it over, in the other. Be careful not to poke a hole in the wall of the chop and to leave about a quarter-inch margin of meat along the chop's outer edge. Fill the chop with stuffing by using a pastry tube or a small funnel.

6 double thick (1 1/2-inch) center-cut
   loin pork chops, tenderloin removed
   (save it for another meal)
1/4 pound bulk country-style sausage
1/4 cup diced bits of any cured
   sausage such as pepperoni, salami,
   summer sausage, or beef stick
1 tablespoon minced onion
1 teaspoon ground ginger root
1/2 cup dried bread crumbs
1 teaspoon chopped parsley
2 tablespoons dry white wine
Salt and freshly ground black pepper
2 tablespoons olive oil

1. Prepare the pockets in the chops.
2. Combine all the remaining ingredients except the oil and mix together well. Stuff the chops.
3. Brush the chops with the oil, dust with salt and pepper, lace on a broiling rack, and bake, uncovered, in a pre-heated 25° F. oven for about 45 minutes. Baste frequently with the pan lices to prevent the chops from drying out. (Note: if the slit you made in the chops was sufficiently small there should be no need to skewer them closed. The stuffing will be sealed in by the cooking process.)

Serving suggestion: Wild or long grain brown rice, asparagus spears with butter, a chilled white wine, and tomato and basil salad are perfect accompaniments.

Serves 6.

SAUSAGE SPIEDINI

Spiedini *in Italian means "skewered." Other cultures variously call their skewered dishes kabobs or shish kebabs, among other things, but by any name they are generally Mediterranean in origin. In this area we have a dish called* spiedi *(pronounced sp*ē*edie) which is marinated cubes of lamb skewered and charcoal-broiled. Various theories abound as to its exact origin but the one that seems the most plausible is that Sicilian shepherds, forced by circumstances to eat on the run, concocted the dish. The lambs they tended were now and then sacrificed for a meal, the meat cubed and the herbs and spices which grew wild in abundance pressed into it as much for preservation as for flavor. The cubes were skewered on green sapling sticks and broiled over an open fire. Simple but incredibly delicious! Future generations brought variations of the dish to this country. The name* spiedi *is no doubt a corruption of the Italian* spiedini.

Combinations of meat and vegetables for kebabs or spiedini are limited only by one's imagination but certain combinations by their very nature suggest themselves as perfect culinary marriages. Italian sausages, small onions, green peppers, and mushrooms are perfect go-togethers. Experiment with your own combinations but try this one first.

1 pound hot or sweet Italian-style sausage cut into one-inch pieces
24 (approximately) one-inch onions, peeled
24 (approximately) square pieces of green pepper
24 (approximately) fresh mushroom caps
1/2 cup olive oil
1/4 cup lemon juice
1 teaspoon oregano
1 teaspoon basil
1/2 teaspoon crushed red pepper
1 teaspoon rosemary
1/2 teaspoon crushed mint leaves
1 clove garlic, finely minced
Salt and freshly ground black pepper

1. Put the sausage, onions, pepper squares, and mushrooms in a large pan. Pour on the oil and lemon juice and sprinkle on the remaining ingredients. Mix well.

2. Marinate the mixture overnight in the refrigerator.

3. Alternate pieces of sausage and vegetables on long metal skewers. Reserve the marinade.

4. Broil the spiedini over a hot charcoal fire until the sausage is cooked through and well browned. Baste frequently with the reserved marinade to prevent the vegetables from burning before the sausage is cooked.

Serving suggestion: It may not be the epitome of elegance but a simple and delicious way of eating spiedini is to pull them off the skewer by wrapping a slice of Italian bread around them and then eating as one would a hot dog.

Serves 4-6.

SAUSAGE SPIEDINI
WITH VEAL

This is another variation on the spiedini theme but this time it is an all-meat dish.

1 pound sweet or hot Italian-style sausage cut into one-inch pieces
1 pound veal cubes (one inch) cut from leg, rump, or shoulder
Marinade (see previous recipe)

1. Combine the sausage and veal pieces and combine with the marinade ingredients as in the previous recipe.
2. Skewer alternating pieces of sausage and veal and charcoal broil, basting frequently, until the meat is done.
Serves 4-6.

GRILLED SAUSAGE
WITH WHITE CLAM SAUCE

This dish has become a family tradition on warm summer evenings when something quick, light, and delicious is an absolute necessity. One ordinarily wouldn't think to combine clams and pork sausage but this recipe proves that strange bedfellows can indeed be the best of friends, at least at the dinner table. Try this dish once with a tossed green salad and cold beer or white sangria and you'll become a lifetime devotee.

2 pounds hot or sweet Italian-style sausage links
4 ounces (1 stick) butter
4 cloves minced garlic
1 medium onion, coarsely chopped
1 cup chopped Italian parsley
2 6 1/2-ounce cans minced clams with their juice
Coarsely ground fresh black pepper (use a lot)
2 dozen fresh littleneck clams, scrubbed
Salt to taste
1 pound linguini or other pasta

1. Prepare a charcoal fire and begin grilling the sausages when the coals are covered by grey ash. Plan on the sausages taking about forty-five minutes.
2. Start boiling a large kettle of salted water for cooking the pasta.
3. Melt the butter in a saucepan and add the garlic and onion. Sauté for about ten minutes or until the onion becomes translucent.
4. Add the parsley and the two cans of clams with their juice to the saucepan. Cook over medium heat for about another ten minutes. Add the black pepper.
(Note: make sure someone is tending the sausages on the grill while you are preparing the clam sauce.)
5. Add the scrubbed fresh clams to the sauce, cover, and cook until the clams open.
6. Cook the linguini. Drain, butter, and spread it out on a large platter.
7. Pour the sauce over the linguini, arranging the whole clams on top and place the grilled sausages around the edges. (The timing here is important but can be accomplished with a little forethought.) Aficionados and purists will scream at this suggestion but a little freshly grated Parmesan cheese sprinkled on top of the clam sauce just before serving is absolutely delicious.
Serves 4-6.

BRACCIOLE STUFFED
WITH SAUSAGE

Bracciole *is an Italian dish traditionally made from flank steak. It used to be that flank steaks weren't very popular and you could walk into a supermarket and cart one off for practically nothing. Now that you need an installment loan to buy meat, the flank steak has gone the way of the sirloin and porterhouse. The problem is compounded by the fact that each steer comes equipped with only two small flank steaks. As more people find out what marvelous things can be done with this piece of meat the price will no doubt continue to climb. This dish can be prepared with a thinly sliced round steak but the texture and flavor won't be quite the same. The sausage extends the meat economically and also provides an interesting treat in the center of the meat roll.*

1 one-pound flank or bottom round
   steak
1 teaspoon coarsely ground fresh
   black pepper (lots of black pepper
   is one of the secrets of this dish)
Salt
1/4 cup chopped Italian parsley
2 tablespoons grated Romano or
   Parmesan cheese
1/2 teaspoon crushed red pepper
1 clove minced garlic
2 tablespoons finely chopped onion
1/2 teaspoon oregano
1/2 teaspoon basil
1/2 teaspoon chopped mint leaves
2 links hot Italian-style sausage
Spaghetti sauce

1. With the side of a meat cleaver or a mallet flatten the steak to about a quarter-inch thickness. The meat should be basically rectangularly shaped.
2. Sprinkle all the herbs and spices evenly over the meat.
3. Place the sausages at the narrower end of the steak and roll the meat up jelly roll fashion. As you get toward the end tuck the sides in.
4. Using kitchen twine, tie the roll tightly at about two-inch intervals.
5. Sauté the roll in olive oil until it is browned on all sides.
6. Finish cooking the bracciole in a pot of spaghetti sauce for about 1 1/2 hours or until it is tender. To serve, remove from the sauce and cut in half-inch slices.

Serves 4-6.

Sausage with Vegetables: Soups, Stews and Casseroles

Nowhere is sausage's versatility more evident than in the multitude of ways in which it can be combined with fresh vegetables.

ACORN SQUASH
STUFFED WITH SAUSAGE

This is almost a complete meal in one dish. A tossed green salad is about all that's needed to complete the fixin's.

2 large acorn squash
2 teaspoons brown sugar
1 pound bulk pork sausage
1/2 cup bread crumbs
1 egg, well beaten

1. Cut each squash in half and scrape out the seeds and pith which clings to the flesh.

2. Sprinkle the cavity of each squash with half a teaspoon of brown sugar.

3. Pour a small amount of water in the bottom of a baking pan, put in the squash, and bake, uncovered, in a preheated 375° F. oven for twenty minutes.

4. Meanwhile combine the sausage meat, bread crumbs, and egg. Mix well.

5. At the end of twenty minutes remove the squash from the oven and (carefully so you don't get burned) stuff one-quarter of the sausage mixture into each of the squash halves.

6. Return the squash to the oven and continue to bake for thirty minutes or until the sausage is cooked through and crisp on top.

Serves 4.

CHOUCROUTE

2 tablespoons olive oil
1 large onion, sliced thinly
1 small rack of spareribs (about two
  pounds), cut into individual ribs
5 small, lean smoked loin pork chops
1 quart sauerkraut, drained and
  rinsed
4 cups shredded cabbage
2 cloves of crushed garlic
1 bay leaf
1/2 teaspoon ground cloves
2 cups (approx.) dry white wine
1 1/2 pounds any assorted combination of the following sausages:
  kielbasa, Italian, knockwurst,
  bratwurst, fresh thuringer, or
  hot dogs

Choucroute is French for sauerkraut but it doesn't begin to describe everything that goes into this dish to make it a hearty and delicious repast for a cold winter's evening. It is a showcase for a variety of your homemade sausages.

1. Heat the oil in a large heavy skillet and sauté the onion until translucent. Remove the onion with a slotted spoon and set it aside.

2. Add the spareribs to the skillet and brown them quickly over medium high heat.

3. Turn off the heat and return the onion to the pot. Add all the remaining ingredients except the sausages. Pour in enough wine to cover everything.

4. Cover and simmer this mixture for about three and a half hours or put everything in a large casserole and place, covered, in a pre-heated 325° F. oven for the same amount of time. Check frequently and add more wine if necessary.

5. At the end of three and a half hours add sausages and cook for an additional thirty-five minutes.

Serving suggestion: put the sauerkraut in a large bowl and arrange the meat on top. Serve with boiled potatoes.

Serves 5.

BUBBLE AND SQUEAK

Bubble and Squeak is an old-time English dish traditionally made with beef and cabbage. This recipe uses sausage meat instead as an interesting twist to the sometimes blandish British cuisine.

1 small head (about 1-1 1/2 pounds) cabbage
1 pound bulk country-style sausage or bulk kielbasa
2 tablespoons clarified butter
2 tablespoons flour
1 cup milk
1 small onion, sliced thinly
1 clove of garlic, minced finely
2 teaspoons Worcestershire sauce
Salt and freshly ground black pepper

1. Cut the cabbage into quarters and boil it in salted water until tender. Check for doneness by piercing with a fork in the center. Drain, chop finely, and set aside.

2. Break up the sausage and sauté it in a skillet until it is lightly browned. Remove it with a slotted spoon and set it aside. Discard all but one tablespoon of the drippings.

3. Add the clarified butter to the drippings left in the skillet and over medium heat gradually add the flour, stirring constantly until the mixture is smooth.

4. Add the milk to the skillet and continue stirring until well mixed.

5. Add the minced garlic and onion to the sauce and then the sausage meat. Add the chopped cabbage, Worcestershire sauce, salt and pepper.

6. Place the mixture in a lightly greased casserole and bake, uncovered, in a pre-heated 325° F. oven until the sauce is bubbly, about thirty minutes.

Serves 4.

CREAMED BROCCOLI WITH SUMMER SAUSAGE

Broccoli is a member of the cabbage family and it was first cultivated in Italy at least four hundred years ago. It is extremely rich in vitamins and minerals and, with the protein from the milk, cheese, and sausage in this recipe, it makes a very nutritious meal.

1 1/2 pounds fresh broccoli
1 cup milk
2 cups grated sharp Cheddar cheese
1 cup diced summer sausage (any fully cured dry or semi-dry sausage will do)
1 tablespoon butter
Salt and freshly ground black pepper

1. Prepare the broccoli. Trim the stem ends and soak the broccoli in cold salted water for thirty minutes. (This is in case any little green worms are hiding out in the broccoli, as they have been known to do.) Rinse and drain. Parboil in salted water for eight to ten minutes or until the broccoli is crisp-tender. Remove and drain. Arrange the broccoli in a two-quart casserole.

2. In a saucepan heat the milk and stir in the grated cheese. Stir constantly over medium heat to prevent sticking. Cook until the cheese is melted and forms a thick sauce. Remove from heat.

3. Stir the diced summer sausage into the cheese sauce.

4. Pour the sauce over the broccoli, add salt and pepper, and dot with butter.

5. Bake, uncovered, in a preheated 375° F. oven for fifteen minutes or until the sauce is bubbly and lightly browned on top.

Serves 4.

CASSOULET

Cassoulet is a French casserole which ranks with boeuf bourguignon and coq au vin as among the world's most famous dishes. Traditional versions (there are many) usually use goose or duck fat to give this dish a distinctive flavor but vegetable or olive oil can be substituted. Chickens are usually much cheaper than ducks or geese so substituting chicken also makes sense. This dish is also a good way of showing off your homemade fresh garlic or Polish sausage. This recipe will feed a crowd.

1 duck or chicken
Salt and freshly ground black pepper
1 small onion, studded with four
   cloves
2 cloves of garlic, peeled and crushed
1/2 pound lean ground pork
1/2 pound lean ground lamb
1 pound fresh garlic or Polish sausage
2 large sweet onions, peeled and thinly sliced
2 cloves of garlic, finely minced
1 cup finely chopped celery with tops
1 cup thinly sliced carrots
2 15-ounce cans navy beans
1 cup dry white wine
1 cup tomato juice
1 tablespoon tomato paste
1/2 teaspoon thyme leaves
1 bay leaf
2 tablespoons chopped parsley

1. Rub the duck or chicken inside and out with salt and pepper. Insert the clove-studded onion and the two crushed garlic cloves into the bird's cavity. Roast on a rack in a pre-heated 375° F. oven until done (about 1 1/2 - 2 hours depending upon the size). Cool, remove the meat from the bones, and cut it into serving pieces.

2. In a Dutch oven sauté the ground pork and lamb until it is lightly browned. Remove it with a slotted spoon and set it aside.

3. Sauté the sausage in the drippings until they are well browned. Don't worry about them being done in the center because they will receive additional cooking. Remove the sausages and set them aside.

4. In the drippings sauté the onions, minced garlic, celery, and carrots until they are crisp tender, about ten minutes.

5. Add the navy beans with their juice, the wine, tomato juice, tomato paste, thyme, bay leaf, chopped parsley, and salt and pepper.

6. Return the ground meat and sausages to the pot and bring to a simmer.

7. Add the pieces of duck or chicken and simmer for fifteen minutes.

8. Transfer the mixture to a large casserole and cook, uncovered, in a pre-heated 375° F. oven for forty-five minutes. Remove the bay leaf (if you can find it) before serving in large bowls.

Serving suggestion: lots of crusty French bread is a must!
Serves 8-10.

BEEF AND SAUSAGE STEW

2 tablespoons vegetable or olive oil
1 pound beef stew meat, cut into one-inch cubes
1 pound link pork sausage
2 cups beef broth
2 cups tomato sauce
1/2 cup dry red wine
2 large potatoes, peeled and diced
2 carrots, scraped and sliced
1 cup green peas (fresh or frozen)
1 cup tiny white onions, peeled
1 tablespoon chopped parsley
Salt and freshly ground black pepper

1. Heat the oil in a Dutch oven and sauté the beef cubes and sausages until they are browned.
2. Add the beef broth, tomato sauce, and wine and simmer gently, covered, for one hour.
3. Add the remaining ingredients and simmer until the vegetables are tender, about thirty minutes. Serve with crusty French bread or over rice.

Serves 4-6.

KIELBASA
WITH GREEN BEANS AND CARROTS

This dish falls in between a soup and a stew. Soup implies more liquid but there's only enough here to hold everything together. Plan on having some fresh, crusty rye bread on hand to sop up the delicious juices when you make this dish.

1 pound fresh kielbasa cut into one-inch pieces
1 small onion, sliced thinly
1 cup dry white wine
2 cups water
2 cups Italian (Romano) green beans, cut into one-inch pieces
2 cups carrots, scraped and sliced
1 bay leaf
2 tablespoons chopped parsley
1 teaspoon paprika
Salt and freshly ground black pepper

1. Put the kielbasa into a heavy pot with just enough water to cover the bottom. Cook over medium heat until the sausage gives up some of its grease and is lightly browned, about ten minutes.
2. Add the onion and cook about five minutes or until the onion is translucent.
3. Add the remaining ingredients and cook for about forty minutes or until the vegetables are tender. Remove the bay leaf. Serve in bowls.

Serves 4.

KIELBASA WITH SWEET CABBAGE

In Polish, capusta *means cabbage, and here's another way to prepare it with Polish sausage.*

2 tablespoons bacon grease or vegetable oil
1 large onion, peeled and chopped
1 pound smoked kielbasa, cut into one-inch pieces
1 small head of cabbage, shredded
1 cup tomato juice
Salt and freshly ground black pepper

1. Heat the grease in a large pot and sauté the onion until it is translucent, about ten minutes.
2. Add the kielbasa and sauté for three minutes.
3. Add the remaining ingredients, cover, and cook for one hour. Adjust heat so that the liquid barely simmers. Serve with rye bread or over boiled potatoes.

Serves 4.

HOLUPKI

Holupki *is a dish of Slavic origin which consists of rolls of stuffed cabbage leaves baked in a tomato sauce. They are traditional at Easter but certainly can be enjoyed anytime. Americans familiar with holupki sometimes call them "pigs in a blanket" (not to be confused with the entirely different dish of the same name, hot dogs wrapped in bread dough and baked). Holupki are at their best if they are made the day before eating and reheated. This recipe is my mother's. She makes it in voluminous quantities at Easter, but I've cut the volume down somewhat so that you can make it at other than festive occasions when large quantities aren't needed. If you would like a larger batch, double or triple the recipe and put some up for freezing.*

1 head cabbage
2 tablespoons vegetable oil
1 medium onion, chopped
1 cup cooked rice
1 1/2 pounds sausage stuffing
  (1 pound ground beef, 1/2 pound
  ground pork, 1 1/2 teaspoon salt,
  1 teaspoon finely ground black
  pepper)
2 10 1/2-ounce cans condensed cream
  of tomato soup plus two soup cans
  water

1. Core the cabbage and place it in a large pot of rapidly boiling salted water. Boil until the cabbage leaves begin to fall apart from each other. (The time will vary according to how young the cabbage is.) Remove the cabbage and set it aside until it is cool enough to handle.

2. In a small skillet sauté the onion in the vegetable oil until it is crisp-tender, about five minutes.

3. Cook the rice according to package directions.

4. In a large bowl mix together the sautéed onion, rice, and the sausage stuffing.

5. Pull apart the cabbage leaves. Cut out the tough center stem in each one.

6. Place a scant quarter-cup of the sausage and rice mixture on one end of a leaf and roll it up, tucking in the sides to enclose the stuffing. Repeat until all the ingredients are used.

7. Mix one can of tomato soup with one can of water and pour it into the bottom of a roasting pan. Place the holupki in a single layer in the pan. Combine the remaining can of soup with a can of water and pour it over the holupki.

8. Bake, covered, for about an hour in a pre-heated 375° F. oven. At this point you can either serve the holupki or, better yet, cool and refrigerate them overnight and reheat them in the oven before serving.

Serves 4-6.

LEEK AND SAUSAGE CASSEROLE

Leeks are not as popular as they ought to be. Members of the onion family, leeks are usually served simply as a braised vegetable or as the principal ingredient in that famous French soup, vichyssoise.

This recipe combines the delicate flavor of leeks with any bulk fresh sausage you have. Crumbled kielbasa and country sausage are especially well suited to this combination.

1 pound bulk sausage
10 medium leeks
3/4 cup grated Swiss, Cheddar, or Gruyère cheese
Dash of cayenne
Salt and freshly ground black pepper

1. Crumble the sausage in a skillet and cook until lightly browned. Remove it with a slotted spoon.
2. Prepare the leeks. Cut off the green tops to within two inches of the white part. Rinse under cold water. Cook in boiling salted water until crisp-tender, about fifteen minutes. Drain.
3. Arrange the leeks in the bottom of a lightly greased baking dish. Layer the cooked sausage on top of the leeks. Sprinkle the grated cheese evenly over the sausage. Add cayenne, salt, and pepper.
4. Place in a pre-heated broiler until the cheese melts and begins to brown lightly on top, about ten minutes.
Serves 4.

EGGPLANT PARMESAN

Eggplant Parmesan is usually a meatless dish but with the addition of sweet Italian-style sausage it becomes a filling and well-balanced meal. Some recipes call for breading the eggplant before frying it but this is an unnecessary step which adds extra calories. If you wish to bread it, however, use the egg wash and seasoned bread crumb mixture you used for City Chicken Sausage Skewers.

1 medium eggplant
1 cup flour seasoned with salt and pepper
1/4 cup clarified butter
1 pound bulk sweet Italian-style sausage
4 cups tomato sauce
12 ounces grated mozzarella cheese
1/4 cup grated Parmesan cheese
1 tablespoon olive oil
Salt and freshly ground black pepper

1. Prepare the eggplant. Wash it under cold running water, dry and slice it into quarter-inch slices.
2. Dust the eggplant slices with the seasoned flour.
3. Pour the butter into a large skillet. Sauté the eggplant, a few slices at a time (don't crowd), until they are golden brown. Drain on paper towels and set them aside. Keep warm.
4. Sauté the sausage in a skillet until it is lightly browned. Remove it with a slotted spoon and keep it warm.
5. Spread a thin layer of the tomato sauce over the bottom of a baking pan. Arrange about half the eggplant slices in the pan. Layer half the sausage over the eggplant followed by half the mozzarella and Parmesan cheeses. Add another layer of sauce and repeat with eggplant, sausage, and cheeses. End with a layer of sauce. Dribble the olive oil over the top.
6. Bake, covered, in a pre-heated 375° F. oven for thirty minutes. Remove the cover and bake an additional ten minutes.
Serves 4-6.

MINESTRONE

Minestre means soup in Italian. Minestrone is a soup loaded with vegetables. When we make minestrone we use homemade sausage to add flavor and richness to the stock.

2 tablespoons olive oil
1 pound sweet Italian-style sausage
  links cut into one-inch pieces
2 carrots, scraped and cut into
  quarter-inch slices
2 celery stalks, sliced quarter-inch
  thick
1 small five-inch zucchini, sliced
1 medium onion, chopped
2 cloves minced garlic
4 tomatoes, peeled, cored, seeded,
  and chopped
1/4 teaspoon thyme
1/4 teaspoon sage
Water
1 cup green peas
1 small can chick peas with their
  liquid
1 cup small macaroni shells
Salt and freshly ground black pepper
1 tablespoon chopped parsley
Parmesan cheese, grated

1. Heat the olive oil in a large pot and brown the sausages.
2. Add the carrots, celery, zucchini, onion, garlic, tomatoes, thyme, and sage. Bring to a simmer. Add about three quarts of water and bring to a boil. Reduce heat to a simmer. Cook, uncovered, for two hours.
3. Add the green peas, chick peas with their liquid, macaroni shells, salt, pepper and parsley. Simmer an additional ten minutes, or until shells are tender.
4. Serve hot with grated Parmesan cheese to pass.
Serves 4-8, depending on whether it is served as a main dish or appetizer.

BRATWURST WITH GERMAN POTATO SALAD

A picnic, in my younger days, always meant my grandfather's German potato salad. To this day the recipe is a family favorite and if you try it once I think you'll understand why.

3 tablespoons vegetable oil
1 pound bratwurst
7 large potatoes, boiled, peeled, and
  sliced
1 large onion, peeled, and thinly
  sliced
1/4 cup cider vinegar
Salt and coarse freshly ground black
  pepper

1. Sauté the bratwurst in the vegetable oil until they are browned and cooked through, twenty-five minutes. Set aside and keep warm.
2. In a large serving bowl mix together the sliced potatoes and onion.
3. Slice the bratwurst into bite-size pieces and add to the potatoes and onions. Add about one-quarter cup of the drippings from the sausage pan. If you don't have enough drippings make up the difference with vegetable oil.
4. Add the vinegar, salt and pepper. Mix and taste for seasoning. Adjust if necessary. This dish may be served hot or cold.
Serves 4.

PAELLA

Paella is a Spanish rice dish for company. Your homemade chorizos give this recipe a solid foundation which is accented by the chicken and seafood. This recipe makes enough for eight people.

1 two-pound lobster
1/2 cup olive oil
2 three-pound frying chickens
3 cloves finely minced garlic
1 large chopped onion
1 pound chorizos, cut into one-inch pieces
1 cup diced ham
1 chopped sweet green pepper
1 teaspoon capers (the brined, not salted, variety)
2 cups crushed tomatoes
2 cups uncooked rice
1 big pinch saffron
1 cup water
1 small jar pimientos
1 teaspoon oregano
1 teaspoon ground coriander
Dash of cayenne
1 pound cooked shrimp
12-24 steamed clams
1 cup fresh or frozen peas cooked until crisp-tender

If you can, in good conscience, afford all these ingredients, then here we go....

1. Boil the lobster in a large pot of water for fifteen minutes. When the lobster is cool enough to handle, remove the meat from the shell.

2. Cut the frying chicken into serving pieces and fry in the olive oil until it is golden brown. Use a large heavy pot or Dutch oven.

3. Add the garlic, onion, chorizos, ham, pepper, and capers. Cook about ten minutes.

4. Add the tomatoes, rice, saffron, water, pimientos, oregano, coriander, cayenne, and shrimp. Mix and cook, covered, about twenty-five minutes or until the liquid is absorbed by the rice. Add the lobster meat, clams, and peas. Heat and serve.

Serves 8.

SAUSAGE AND LENTILS

This dish is both hearty and quick to prepare.

1 pound Polish- or Italian-style sausage cut into one-inch pieces
1 large sweet onion, sliced thinly
1 teaspoon crushed mint leaves
6 cups water
1 cup dry white wine
2 cups dry lentils
1 teaspoon lemon or orange zest
1 tablespoon chopped parsley
1 tablespoon tomato paste
Salt and freshly ground black pepper

1. In a large heavy pot brown the sausage pieces lightly. Start with a little water to get the grease flowing freely from the sausage.

2. Add the onion and sauté until it is translucent, about five minutes.

3. Add the remaining ingredients and bring to a boil. Reduce heat so that the liquid simmers gently. Cover and cook for about an hour. Serve hot in bowls.

Serves 4.

SAUSAGE AND BEAN CASSEROLE

This is a quick one-dish meal which is as delicious as it is nutritious.

2 16-ounce cans pork and beans in
   tomato sauce
1 small onion, chopped
1 sweet green pepper cored, seeded,
   and chopped
1/4 cup ketchup
2 tablespoons prepared mustard
1 pound homemade sausage links (any
   variety)

1. Mix together the first five ingredients.
2. Cut up sausage links into one-inch pieces and stir into bean mixture.
3. Bake, covered, in a pre-heated 375° F. oven for about one hour.

Serves 4.

SAUSAGE AND CORN ONE-DISH SUPPER

You've probably at one time or another had a baked casserole dish of creamed corn spiced with green peppers. This is a variation on that theme with the added benefit of the protein derived from sausage, making it an economical and quick one-dish meal. You can vary the kind of sausage used as well as some of the other ingredients to suit your own tastes. For a mild version use country-style sausage or any of the Vienna-style sausages. For a Mexican theme use chorizos and chopped green chilies. If you opt for the latter version be sure to have a fire extinguisher (or at least lots of cold beer) handy for putting out the flames.

1 tablespoon olive or vegetable oil
1 pound country-style, Vienna, or
   chorizo sausages
4 tablespoons butter
1/4 cup chopped onion
1/4 cup flour
2 cups milk
2 16-ounce cans corn or 4 cups of
   fresh or frozen corn parboiled for
   five minutes
1 sweet green pepper, seeded, cored,
   and coarsely chopped *or* 1/4 cup
   chopped green chili peppers
1/4 cup chopped pimiento strips
Salt and freshly ground black pepper
1 1/2 cups cracker crumbs

1. Cut the sausage into one-inch pieces and brown quickly in the oil in a large skillet. Remove with a slotted spoon and set aside. Drain off the grease.
2. Melt the butter in the skillet and sauté the onion until it is translucent.
3. Add the flour and milk to the skillet and stir constantly to prevent burning.
4. Return the sausage to the skillet and add the corn. Mix well. Add the peppers, pimiento, salt and pepper.
5. Layer a greased casserole with one-third of the cracker crumbs and top with one-third of the sausage and corn mixture. Layer twice more, reserving a tiny bit of crumbs for the top layer.
6. Bake, uncovered, in a pre-heated 350° F. oven for twenty-five minutes or until the casserole is bubbly and browned on top.

Serves 4.

SAUSAGE AND GREENS

Just like robins, one of the first harbingers of spring is dandelions. While most people are out on their lawns fighting a losing battle trying to eradicate them we're out there picking the greens for our next meal. Some people prefer the more bitter dandelion greens of early to mid-summer but we like the tender young leaves of early spring. If you care to harvest your own dandelions confine your picking to wide open spaces away from roads, parking lots, and any place near civilization. Highway crews often spray near roads to eradicate weeds and car exhausts lace the greenery near roads with lead and other pollutants. Unless the greens you use are the cultured variety (yes — some people do plant them) which can be quite large, you'll need about a grocery bag full of them to make this dish worthwhile. This recipe can also be prepared with green beet tops, curly endive, or any of these in combination.

2 tablespoons olive oil
1 pound sweet Italian-style or fresh garlic sausage cut into one-inch pieces
Lots of dandelion or other greens
2 tablespoons tomato sauce
Grated Parmesan cheese to taste
Salt and freshly ground black pepper

1. Sauté the sausage in the olive oil in a large pot until well browned. Remove the sausage with a slotted spoon.

2. Wash the greens well and drain. Add them to the pot, cover, and cook over medium heat until they are tender, about fifteen minutes.

3. Return the sausage to the pot and add the tomato sauce, Parmesan cheese, salt and pepper. Heat through and serve.

Serves 4 as a side dish.

SAUSAGE AND VEGETABLE CURRY

You can use either fresh garlic or chorizo sausages for this recipe or experiment with some other variety.

3 tablespoons peanut oil
2 pounds fresh sausage links cut into one-inch pieces
1 small onion, chopped
1 carrot, scraped and thinly sliced
4 cups fresh Romano green beans, cut into one-inch pieces
1 teaspoon red pepper flakes
2 teaspoons (or to taste) curry powder (or your own blend of coriander, turmeric, cumin, mace, and pepper)
Buttered rice

1. Heat the oil in a large skillet and brown the sausage pieces.

2. Add the onion and carrot and sauté until the carrot is crisp-tender.

3. Add the beans, red pepper, and curry powder, stirring over medium high heat, about ten minutes or until the beans are crisp-tender. Serve over hot buttered rice.

Serves 4.

SAUSAGE AND PEAS
WITH TOMATO SAUCE

Every year we have a contest to see who gets the first baby pod of peas from the garden. The first peas of early spring are the tenderest and sweetest either because they really are or because it has been a year since the last fresh peas were plucked from the vine and popped into the mouth. After everyone at your house has had his fill of peas you might want to try some in this dish. It combines the hardiness requisite for those sometimes nippy early spring evenings with the freshness and sweetness of nature's reawakening.

2 tablespoons olive oil
1 pound sweet Italian-style sausage links cut into one-inch pieces
3 cups ditalini macaroni
2 cups shelled fresh peas (or substitute frozen)
3 cups tomato sauce
1 teaspoon crushed mint leaves
3 fresh basil leaves
Salt and freshly ground black pepper
1 tablespoon chopped parsley

1. Heat the oil in a heavy skillet and brown the sausages.
2. Bring four quarts of water to boil and add macaroni.
3. Steam the peas for four minutes or until crisp-tender.
4. Add the tomato sauce to the skillet with the sausage and bring to a simmer. Add the peas, mint, basil, parsley, and salt and pepper. Simmer gently while you cook the macaroni.
5. When the macaroni is *al dente* (still slightly firm), drain and add it to the simmering sauce. Mix well. Garnish with chopped parsley. Serve hot with crusty French bread and a tossed green salad.
Serves 4-6.

SAUSAGE GOULASH

Goulash is generally thought to be strictly a Hungarian dish but all Slavic countries have their own versions of this delectable stew. Use any mildly spiced German-, French-, or Italian-style sausage for this recipe.

2 tablespoons olive oil
1 pound fresh sausage links, cut into one-inch pieces
2 large sweet onions, sliced very thinly
2 cloves crushed garlic (you may want to omit these if you are using a garlicky sausage)
4 cups water
2 tablespoons paprika
1 tablespoon chopped parsley
Salt and freshly ground black pepper
Cooked rice or rye bread

1. Heat the oil in a Dutch oven and sauté the sausage pieces until they are lightly browned. Remove the meat and keep warm.
2. Sauté the onion and garlic until the onion is translucent, about ten minutes.
3. Put the meat back in the pot, add the water, paprika, parsley, salt and pepper. Simmer gently for about thirty minutes.
4. If you are serving rice, prepare it while the goulash is cooking.
5. Serve steaming hot in large bowls over rice or with rye bread.
Serves 4.

SAUSAGE HASH

The word hash has evil connotations for many people because it conjures up thoughts of leftovers that should have been left to rest. It needn't be so. There is nothing leftover about this recipe (unless of course you make too much). Vary the flavor by using any variety of fresh sausage.

4 cups (about 1 pound) fresh sausage, removed from the casing
1/2 cup chopped onion
4 cups peeled, cooked, and chopped potatoes
1/2 cup cooked chopped carrots
Hot fat for frying

1. Sauté the sausage until it is lightly browned.
2. Sauté the onion in the sausage drippings until it is translucent, about ten minutes.
3. Add the potaotes and carrots to the sausage and mix well. Form the mixture into patties and brown in hot fat.
Serves 4.

SAUSAGE PAPRIKASH

Paprikash means "made with paprika" — usually lots of it. Unfortunately the paprika to which most Americans are accustomed is nothing at all like the real thing. Hungarian paprika comes in a spectrum of flavors ranging from mild and sweet to extremely pungent. One thing that all Hungarian varieties have in common and the thing that most American varieties lack, is flavor. Many people, therefore, think of paprika basically as a coloring agent when it should be a flavoring agent.

2 tablespoons clarified butter
2 pounds kielbasa or German fresh sausage links, cut into one-inch pieces
2 large sweet onions, peeled, quartered, and thinly sliced
4 cups beef or veal stock
1 twelve-ounce can beer or ale
3 tablespoons paprika
1/2 cup chopped parsley
Salt and freshly ground black pepper
Buttered noodles

1. Heat the butter in a Dutch oven and sauté the sausage until browned.
2. Add the onion, stock, beer, and paprika. Simmer, uncovered, for thirty minutes.
3. Add the parsley and over medium high heat slowly add the flour until the mixture thickens. Stir constantly. Add salt and pepper. Serve hot over buttered noodles.
Serves 4.

SCALLOPED POTATOES
WITH SAUSAGE

Any spicy fresh sausage such as kielbasa is good in this recipe.

6 large potatoes
3 tablespoons butter
2 tablespoons flour
3 cups milk
Dash of cayenne
Salt and freshly ground black pepper
1 onion, sliced very thinly
1 pound fresh sausage, cut into one-
inch slices

1. Scrub and peel the potatoes. Rinse and slice thinly.
2. In a saucepan melt the butter and mix in the flour to make a *roux*. Add the milk, a little at a time, and beat with a whisk to blend. Add a dash of cayenne and salt and pepper.
3. In a greased casserole layer the potatoes, onion, sauce, and sliced sausage. Begin and end with a layer of sauce.
4. Bake, covered, in a pre-heated 425° F. oven for sixty minutes. Uncover and brown the top.
Serves 4.

STIR FRY SAUSAGE
AND VEGETABLES

This is a Chinese-style dish which is extremely nutritious and can be prepared quickly. My sister deserves credit for the basic recipe but I've taken the liberty of adjusting it to accommodate some of your homemade sausages. If you have a wok use it to cook this dish.

1 1/2 tablespoons peanut oil
2 cloves of crushed garlic
2 teaspoons freshly ground ginger
1 pound mild pork sausage links, cut
into one-inch pieces
4 carrots, scraped and thinly sliced
2 sweet green peppers, cored, seeded,
and cut into strips
4 green onions, cut into half-inch
pieces
2 1/2 cups coarsely shredded cabbage
1 cup sliced celery

Optional ingredients:
Bean sprouts
Fresh mushrooms
Bamboo shoots
Water chestnuts
Fresh spinach
Fresh broccoli
Fresh cauliflower
1 tablespoon cornstarch
2 tablespoons soy sauce
2 tablespoons Worcestershire sauce
Cooked rice

1. Heat the peanut oil in a large heavy skillet or a wok. Add the garlic and sauté it until it begins to turn brown (don't burn it). Remove it. Add the ground ginger. When the ginger begins to bubble in the oil add the sausage pieces and sauté them until they are browned. Remove the sausage with a slotted spoon. Keep it warm.
2. Add more oil if necessary and add the vegetables, stirring constantly over high heat until they are crisp-tender. Add the vegetables in order of *descending* time needed to cook (i.e. the carrots go in before the mushrooms because they take longer to cook).
3. Return the sausage to the skillet.
4. Combine the cornstarch with the soy sauce and Worcestershire sauce and pour this mixture over the sausage and vegetables, stirring constantly until the mixture is glazed. Serve hot over cooked rice.
Serves 4-6.

SAUSAGE WITH ONIONS, PEPPERS, AND MUSHROOMS IN WINE SAUCE

This recipe makes an excellent buffet dish for a party. It's easy and quick to prepare and can be scooped into party rolls to be eaten out of hand.

2 pounds hot Italian-style sausage
Olive oil
2 large sweet onions, sliced thinly
2 large red or green sweet peppers cored, seeded, and cut into strips
1 pound fresh mushrooms, sliced thinly
1 cup dry white wine

1. In a large skillet sauté the sausage in a little olive oil until it is well browned. Remove it with a slotted spoon and set it aside.
2. In the drippings sauté the onions and peppers until they are crisp-tender. Remove with a slotted spoon and set aside.
3. Sauté mushrooms until they give up most of their liquid.
4. Cut the sausage into half-inch slices and return it to the skillet along with the onions and peppers.
5. Add the wine and cook over medium heat until the liquid is almost evaporated.
Serves 4-6.

SPANISH RICE WITH CHORIZOS

2 slices of diced bacon
1 pound fresh chorizo sausages, cut into one-inch pieces
1 medium onion, chopped
1 sweet green pepper, seeded, cored, and chopped
2 cups tomato sauce
1 cup uncooked rice
Salt and freshly ground black pepper

1. Cook the bacon until crisp and remove it from the skillet.
2. Add the chorizos to the bacon grease and sauté until well browned. Remove them from the pan with a slotted spoon.
3. Cook the onion and pepper until they are crisp-tender. Drain off all but two tablespoons of the drippings.
4. Return the bacon and chorizos to the pan, add the tomato sauce, and bring to a simmer.
5. Cook the rice according to package directions.
6. Add the rice to the skillet, mix well, and serve at once.
Serves 4.

TEXAS-STYLE SAUSAGE CHILI

This is real Texas-style chili with lots of kidney beans in a hot, spicy sauce and enough meat to make any Texan brag. You can use either bulk country-style sausage or (preferably) fresh chorizos removed from the casing and crumbled.

1 pound bulk sausage
2 cloves garlic, minced
1 medium onion, chopped
3 tablespoons chili powder (or substitute your own combination of spices such as ground chilis, cumin, coriander, fenugreek, and oregano)
1 28-ounce can kidney beans
2 cups tomato puree
Salt and freshly ground pepper

1. Sauté the sausage meat until it is lightly browned.
2. Add the garlic and onion and cook ten minutes.
3. Add the chili powder, beans, tomato puree, salt and pepper. Simmer about forty-five minutes or until thickened.
Serves 4.

SWEDISH MEATBALLS
AND SAUSAGE

1 ring Swedish sausage (Potatis Korv)
2 tablespoons vegetable oil
1/2 cup finely chopped onion
1/2 pound ground beef
1/2 pound ground pork
1/2 pound ground veal
1 cup fresh bread crumbs
1 clove very finely minced garlic
1/8 teaspoon nutmeg
1/8 teaspoon allspice
1 tablespoon chopped parsley
2 eggs, well beaten
Salt and freshly ground black pepper
Shortening for frying
1 10-ounce can cream of mushroom
    soup
1/2 cup dry white wine
1/2 cup water

1. Boil the sausage in a large pot for forty-five minutes. Remove, pat dry, and set aside.

2. Assemble the meatballs by sautéing the chopped onion in the vegetable oil until it is translucent. Combine the drained onion with the beef, pork, veal, bread crumbs, garlic, nutmeg, allspice, parsley, eggs, salt and pepper. Mix with your hands and shape into one-inch meatballs.

3. Sauté the meatballs in hot shortening until they are well browned. Remove with a slotted spoon and set aside.

4. Slice the sausage into bite-sized pieces and sauté quickly in the same skillet used for the meatballs just until it is lightly browned. Drain all but one tablespoon of grease from the skillet.

5. Return the meatballs to the skillet. Add the cream of mushroom soup, wine, and water to the skillet and heat over medium heat until the mixture bubbles. Serve hot in large bowls.
    Serves 4-6.

SPANISH SAUSAGE SOUP

This soup is hot and spicy, rich with the flavor of chorizos. For a change of pace you can substitute other varieties of sausage in this recipe.

2 tablespoons olive oil
1 pound fresh sausage links, cut into
    one-inch pieces
2 large potatoes, peeled and diced
1 carrot, scraped and sliced
1 celery stalk with top, chopped
1 large onion, chopped
1 10-ounce package frozen baby lima
    beans
2 quarts chicken or beef stock
2 tablespoons tomato paste
Salt and freshly ground black pepper

1. Heat the olive oil in a large pot and sauté the sausages until they are lightly browned.

2. Add the potatoes, carrot, celery, and onion to the pot and sauté for about ten minutes.

3. Add the lima beans, stock, tomato paste, salt and pepper. Simmer, uncovered, for an hour. Serve hot.
    Serves 4.

ZUCCHINI STUFFED
WITH SAUSAGE

It happens every year. We plan, plant, nurture, and sweat over our garden until one day it bursts forth with a bounty of fresh young tender vegetables. It also always happens that we eat our fill, put up as much as our pantry shelves and freezer can hold, give away to our neighbors as much as we can before they begin avoiding us, and we still have something left over.

More often than not that something is zucchini. That's after we've had our fill of fried zucchini, zucchini bread, boiled and buttered zucchini, zucchini pickles, zucchini this and zucchini that. It's not that we plant so much zucchini, it's just that once zucchini vines start producing they don't know when to stop. Consequently we're always looking for new ways to fix this tasty Italian summer squash. Here's one recipe that we're particularly fond of because it provides a variety of different textures and flavors centered around this one prolific vegetable.

1 medium large zucchini
3 links sweet Italian-style sausage,
   removed from from the casing
1/4 cup finely chopped onion
2 cloves garlic, minced
1/4 pound chopped fresh mushrooms
1 6-ounce can tomato paste
1/4 cup dry white wine
1/4 cup grated Romano cheese
2 tablespoons chopped parsley
Salt and freshly ground black pepper
Parmesan cheese
Olive oil

1. In a pot large enough to hold the zucchini and water to cover, boil the water and add the whole zucchini. Return to a boil and reduce heat so that the water simmers. Cook for ten minutes. Remove the zucchini, pat dry, and set aside.

2. In a skillet crumble the sausage and sauté until it loses its pink color. Add the onion, garlic, and mushrooms and sauté an additional five minutes over medium heat. Remove from heat.

3. Slice the zucchini in half lengthwise. Scoop out the flesh with a spoon. Be careful not to puncture the skin. Leave about a half-inch of flesh in the skin. Chop the removed flesh and add it to the sausage mixture.

4. Add the tomato paste, wine, cheese, parsley, salt and pepper. Return to heat and warm the mixture through.

5. Lightly grease a baking pan with the olive oil and place the hollowed-out zucchini halves in the pan. Divide the sausage mixture between the halves. Sprinkle a small amount of Parmesan cheese on each zucchini, dribble a little olive oil on each, and bake in a pre-heated 350° F. oven for thirty minutes or until the zucchini is tender and the filling is bubbling.

Serves 4.

VEAL AND SAUSAGE
STEW A LA MARSALA

This concoction both pleases the eye and devilishly tickles the palate. It is a veal and sausage version of beef bourguignon with a subtly herbed sauce to accent the mildly sweet meat. This dish is started in a large skillet and finished in a three-quart casserole in the oven.

4 tablespoons clarified butter
2 tablespoons finely minced shallots
2 cloves crushed garlic
3/4 pound fresh sliced mushrooms
1 cup Marsala
1/4 cup flour
2 pounds veal, cut into one-inch cubes
1 pound sweet Italian-style sausage
    links cut into one-inch pieces
2 tablespoons clarified butter
1 1/2 cups beef broth
1 large sweet onion, chopped
1 red and one green sweet pepper,
    cored, seeded, and chopped
2 large potatoes, peeled and cut into
    bite-sized pieces
2 cups crushed tomatoes
1 tablespoon dill weed, chopped
1/2 teaspoon thyme
1/2 teaspoon oregano
1 tablespoon orange liqueur
1 bay leaf
2 tablespoons flour
1/4 cup parsley, chopped
Salt and freshly ground black pepper

1. In four tablespoons of the clarified butter sauté the shallots, garlic, and mushrooms until crisp-tender, about five minutes. Add the Marsala and reduce the liquid by half over high heat. Pour into a three-quart casserole.

2. Dredge the veal in a quarter-cup flour. Sauté the veal and sausage pieces in two tablespoons of clarified butter until the sausage and veal are browned.

3. Add the remaining ingredients except the parsley and remaining flour. Cook over medium heat for about five minutes to blend the flavors. Bring the mixture to a boil and sprinkle in two tablespoons of flour, stirring constantly.

4. Add this mixture to the casserole and stir into the mushroom mixture.

5. Cover and place in a pre-heated 350° F. oven for one hour. Before serving sprinkle on the parsley and remove the bay leaf.

Serving suggestion: crusty French bread, a tossed green salad, and a young red wine go very well.

Serves 6-8.

TOMATO SAUCE WITH PEPPERONI,
SOPPRESATTA OR SALAMI

This sauce is excellent on top of your favorite pasta or, used judiciously, as a substitute for regular tomato sauce in many recipes.

1 tablespoon olive oil
1/2 pound pepperoni, soppresatta or
    salami cut into a quarter-inch dice
4 cups basic tomato sauce
1/4 cup grated Parmesan cheese
1 teaspoon chopped parsley

1. Heat the oil in a saucepan and sauté the diced sausage for two to three minutes.

2. Add the tomato sauce and bring to a simmer.

3. Stir in the cheese and parsley. Simmer an additional ten minutes. Serve over freshly cooked pasta or use in a recipe calling for tomato sauce.

BASIC TOMATO SAUCE

There are more recipes for spaghetti sauce than there are seats in Yankee Stadium. If you have your own favorite you might want to stick with it, but this recipe is one that can be expanded and is perfectly suited to any recipe in this book which requires a tomato sauce. It freezes beautifully so make more than you need.

2 tablespoons olive oil
3 links sweet Italian-style sausage
1 pound pork spareribs or pork neck
  bones
2 beef short ribs
2 pounds veal bones
1/2 cup chopped onion
4 cloves of garlic, minced
1 carrot, scraped and shredded
3 quarts tomato puree
1/2 cup water
1/2 cup dry white wine
2 six-ounce cans tomato paste
2 teaspoons fresh chopped basil leaves
  or 1/2 teaspoon dry
1 large sprig fresh oregano
1 teaspoon chopped mint leaves
2 tablespoons chopped parsley
Salt and freshly ground black pepper

1. Heat the olive oil in a large pot and brown the sausage, pork, beef, and veal bones. Remove.

2. Sauté the onion, garlic, and carrot for ten minutes or until tender.

3. Add the puree, water, and wine and return the bones and sausage to the pot. Simmer, uncovered, very slowly for about two hours.

4. Remove the sausage and bones (they're delicious to gnaw on). Put the sauce through a food mill, blender, or food processor. Return it to the pot.

5. Add the tomato paste and all remaining ingredients. Simmer, uncovered, for thirty minutes. Makes about 3 1/2 quarts.

Suppliers

The following is a list of sources for sausage-making supplies. Not all the firms listed carry all the items necessary for making sausage. Most firms will send you a free catalogue.

Cook's Mart, 609 N. LaSalle St., Chicago, Illinois 60610. Stuffers, grinders.

The Cuisine Marketplace, 133B W. DeLaGuerra, Santa Barbara, California 93101. Herbs and spices.

Deer Valley Farm, R.D. #1, Guilford, New York 13780. Herbs and spices.

Gary Valenti, 55-72 61 Street, Maspeth, New York 11378. Grinders.

H. Roth and Son, 1577 First Avenue, New York, New York 10028. Grinders, casings.

J. A. Henkels Twinworks, Inc., 1Westchester Plaza, Elmsford, New York 10523. Knives.

Mouli Manufacturing Company, 1 Montgomery Street, Belleville, New Jersey 07109. Grinders.

Paprikâs Weiss, 1546 Second Avenue, New York, New York 10028. Herbs and spices.

R. H. Forschner Company, Inc., 324 Lafayette Street, New York, New York 10012. Knives.

Richard S. Kutas Company, 1067 Grant Street, Buffalo, New York 14207. Grinders, stuffers, casings, preservatives, premixed seasonings, recipes.

Rowoco, 111 Calvert Street, Harrison, New York 10528. Grinders.

Schiller and Asmus, Inc., 1525 Merchandise Mart, Chicago, Illinois 60654. Grinders.

Sedro Industries, P.O. Box 8009, Rochester, New York 14606. Casings.

The Standard Casing Company, Inc., 121 Spring Street, New York, New York 10012. Casings.

Tartarowicz's, 390 Broadway, Bayonne, New Jersey 07109. Casings.

Index